FENG SHUI
for the
SOUL

how to achieve more ohm from your home

AMANDA GATES

Approach it and there is no beginning;
　　Follow it and there is no end.
　　You can't know it, but you can be it,
　　At ease in your own life.
　　Just realize where you come from:
　　This is the essence of wisdom.

— TAO TE CHING

TABLE *of* CONTENTS

This book is dedicated to my parents, Troy and Ruthie Hittle. Thank you for all that you do for me.
Thank you for your unbounded support and extraordinary belief in me, especially since I've always been weird.

INTRODUCTION

"Stop chasing a dream that doesn't belong to you. When it comes to finding your purpose you, have to give up the need to know what happens next."
Caroline Myss

In my early twenties, my then-husband and I started work on an older Northern California home built in 1972. It was a dream come true to have a place to set down roots, foster growth, cultivate memories and luxuriate in a place called home. But, unlike most homes, this one had not been loved on in many years. This one had fallen into foreclosure, and to avoid losing his home, the previous homeowner allowed homeless people to occupy the space, deeming them "renters." According to the state laws at the time, as long as residents occupied the home, it could not be taken away by the bank—a sort of loophole in the system. Unbeknownst to us, the "bargain" price we paid in order to be in one of the best neighborhoods also came with a lot of negative Chi (energy), but it would also eventually lead me to an enlightened career path.

When we purchased the home, it lacked many things. The kitchen cabinets had been ripped out, there were no appliances, and a random stove had been placed in the middle of a room with a large hole cut into the ceiling. It was a bit extreme but a perfect DIY solution to exhaust the makeshift stove. However, not the best solution to keep out bugs, birds, or rain, unless of course that's what you're going for.

In addition to a random stove in the middle of what we assumed was once a kitchen, all the floors had been ripped out, toilets destroyed, walls punched, and rooms thoroughly urinated on. Despite the filth, that's not how I saw her. This home could be the epitome of refinement and beauty, and despite the lack of love and care given to her, I was determined to bring her back to her glory. Which was a fairly tall order, considering my current career path was in science and lacking of knowledge in anything related to home. But I could see past the destruction, and I was determined to do this. Simultaneously, I was developing a strange bond to an idea called home. This was the start of what would later become known as a Honey Heart in my Feng Shui practice. But more on that later.

Unfortunately, this house didn't level up without a fight. This gal's energy was indignant. And rightfully so. Antagonized, bitter and enraged by the way she had been treated, I could *feel* her sadness. As I write this, it takes me back to those early years of feeling a home's energy, not knowing what it was or how to truly speak the language, but I *felt* it. She had been let down and taken advantage of, and her occupants had not shown her love and appreciation for a very long time. As any good woman can attest, being devalued and under-appreciated will break your spirit, and hers had been destroyed.

This was not a healthy home. This was not a happy home.

When a home is not thoroughly loved on and cared for, it changes her essence. The energy becomes broken, scattered, and disoriented. Stagnant fragments of energy create tight knots in corners that grip like cobwebs, and if you pay attention, you can feel it. In addition to corners, negative pockets, or what I like to call energy cyclones, can easily be found at the kitchen sink, stove, front door, and commonly in the owner's suite. These pockets pick you up like a tornado, whisking you about, and you fall instantly into negative emotions without understanding why.

Homes are a direct reflection of self. When there is a disconnect between you and your home, you lose a sense of self. You feel detached and maybe even indifferent, not realizing that it's the cyclone of negative energy you repeatedly step into night after night, day after day. Unknowingly, you blame yourself for being moody, or take it out on your spouse because you're getting swept up in emotions that don't belong to you. I can't tell you how many times I've heard over the years from clients, "I hate my house," or, "I've never really liked my house." As you'll learn in the next chapter, those thoughts and emotions matter.

Your home is a third skin, an intrinsic part of who you are and how you show up in the world. The words you use and the emotions you experience are absorbed within the walls of your home—an energy residue that's left behind and can always be experienced again. She literally becomes a living, breathing entity of energy that surrounds your most intimate, prized moments, so mistreating her only results in mistreating yourself.

Wait, wait, wait. You're telling me that my house has feelings?

Yep!

Absorbed from you and and all of her visitors. Even the land she was built on has residue. But I know what you're thinking: This sounds crazy! It is, until you experience it. I too was under the impression that I just needed to find a house, make her pretty to impress my in-laws, and maybe knock out Sherry from next door with my new pretty kitchen. Boy, was I in for the surprise of my life!

IT'S ALL ABOUT THE PRETTY, ISN'T IT?

A few months after buying our bargain dream house, we moved in. We worked on the weekends, we worked on it at night, and we worked on it every spare moment we had. We repainted every inch, corner, nook, and cranny. We ripped out the remaining laminate floors, opened up walls, removed a bedroom, added closets, and painted more walls. We replaced the space that once housed a stove with a hole in the ceiling with a beautiful cherry kitchen and granite counters. What emerged was a beautiful one thousand-square-foot kitchen with a ten-foot island that any amateur cook such as myself could dream of, along with an open floor plan, professionally organized closets, sparkling chandeliers, and new wood floors. She was pretty. Time to have the neighbors over, right?

Despite a year of very hard work, new paint, carpet, lighting, cabinets, hardware, and shiny new Kohler toilets, something was off. She wasn't right. I could feel it deep in my bones that my new home was still not right, but I didn't know why or how to fix it. And I'll admit, I also thought I was losing my mind. I was experiencing this weird breathing thing that I later discovered was called panic attacks, and I couldn't explain that either. It didn't matter where I was. Reading before bed, in the middle of the paint aisle at Home Depot, or at lunch with my girlfriends, it would hit me and I could not catch my breath. I once got one so bad at Home Depot, I ended up having to buy a painter's smock because my clothes were covered in tears, spit, and mascara. Not a proud moment!

What was perplexing at this stage of the renovation was most of the interior was complete, and the stuff within our new home was beautiful. You couldn't get prettier than this home. Sparkly chandeliers, trendy tile showers, Brazilian wood floors, brand new bathrooms outfitted in the latest shiny finishes, and a kitchen furnished with everything new from top to bottom. How did this relate to feeling like things were off? She was so *pretty*. And why was I having issues? My doctor said that panic attacks were associated with severe stress and anxiety, of which I felt neither. Or did I? Was I stressed?

Here's where the rubber finally meets the road. While these strange episodes were occurring in my life, the entire front of our house was ripped apart to repair its sagging exterior. For months, we used the back door with no way to access the front entrance because our contractor kept giving us the perpetual, haughty response, "just a few more weeks." It meant nothing to us, as we had plenty to do with the renovation of the interior and, other than a rainy January, and one bout with an infestation of ants inside my car, we hardly saw it as a problem. That was until I realized it was a really big problem.

THE PHYSICAL WORLD AFFECTS YOUR EMOTIONAL WORLD

It was late fall, and I was standing in a Borders bookstore (remember those?) staring at what seemed like a gazillion interior decorating books, confused and uncertain of what to do next. I was paralyzed with fear. But a small part of me figured if I could just make my house more pretty she'd feel better to me. Hell, maybe I'd feel better too. As if I had some cool decorating sonar that would magically fix everything, I was convinced that if I picked the right book, my house would feel better. Good grief, but how do you pick the right book with so many options?

At that moment in time I had just graduated with a degree in Biology and had turned down my acceptance into Western University's medical program in the hopes of applying at U.C. Davis. Given my strong analytical training at the time, I stared at all those fluffy decorating books and quickly realized I was in way over my head. It was happening again; the panic was setting in. My future in medicine was hanging in the balance, I couldn't keep a job to save my life, opportunities that once flooded my life were stifled, and I was so indecisive I couldn't even choose a damn decorating book on how to "pretty up my house" correctly. Damn, I don't have cool decorating sonar after all. *Wait! Is this the stress my doctor spoke of? Perhaps this was the anxiety he mentioned? Wait, seriously?* My left analytical brain went into hyperdrive. *I'm going to have a panic attack over choosing a decorating book? Good lord, I am crazy!*

Without realizing it, I had been standing there for nearly twenty minutes when a woman broke me out of my panic-trance with a sweet smile and a soft hello. She had short, fluffy blonde hair that was tossed but curly. Her eyes were as blue as the sea and, as she looked at me, I could feel her warmth, an indescribable love radiating from her that should have seemed odd from a stranger, but I was transfixed by her light. Little did I know, this woman was about to change my destiny.

"My darling, my dear," she said with a huge smile and a chuckle, "you don't need those books—" pointing at the assortment of fluffy decorating books, "—you need that book!" Pointing towards a book with the strangest "F" word I'd ever seen. (Unbeknownst to me it would soon become my favorite "F" word! Stay tuned; it's gonna become your favorite "F" word, too!)

I was dumbfounded. Cemented and completely rooted in my stance, I stared at her, and all I could muster up was, "I'm sorry?"

"My name is Dr. Marlene, I teach metaphysics at the local college, but I'm also an intuitive and you're in trouble." She said with exasperated excitement and a big smile. "If you don't get that front door fixed more things will come to a halt," she said, shoving a Feng Shui book at me. She followed with, "And you got some not-so-good energy in there darling. Phew! Is it sticky. Bleh!" Spinning around and starting to walk away she turned back around and looked back at me. "Best if you get on that right away," she said pointing and then waving feverishly, she flipped around and quickly walked away.

What the hell just happened? I thought to myself. As I looked down, I was holding Karen Kingston's book, *Creating Sacred Space With Feng Shui.* I flipped through the seemingly ominous "F" word book and picked up another, and another. As I read *The Western Guide to Feng Shui* by Terah Kathryn Collins, my knees hit the floor.

> *In Feng Shui, the front entrance is the largest, most important mouth for Ch'i. It represents your relationship with society and is meant to welcome and direct positive Ch'i in the form of good energy, people and new opportunities. A hindrance creates a reduction in Ch'i flow causing annoyance and irritation, and reduces promising opportunities, resources and circumstances in your life. A hinderance acts as a "booby trap" negatively affecting the Ch'i making it unsafe and rile, rather than soothing.*

I've told this story many times on my blog, podcast, classes and other public channels, but it was at this moment I literally heard the Angels singing and my world starting to make sense again. Mountains moved, the skies cleared, and I felt destiny. And luckily, the panic subsided. It was at this moment I realized I wasn't crazy, and I wasn't making this up from my imagination. I was tapping into something otherworldly through my emotions, and it cemented in me that the physical world affects your emotional world and vice versa. I wasn't experiencing panic attacks due to stress; my home was speaking to me through the only language she knew how: my emotions. Hallelujah, sweet friend, I'm listening!

JOURNEY TO A PLACE CALLED HOME

Marlene would soon become a huge guiding light in my life. After that experience at the bookstore, I realized that the answer to all my prayers, or rather panic attacks, lay in this little but complex energy thing called Feng Shui. I devoured every book I could get my hands on and quickly realized that much of my home was in *energetic* disrepair. The lack of a front door had made both my husband and me a complete mess, not to mention the energetic residue from years of neglect, and low consciousness beings inhabiting her. It's no wonder she was so unhappy. I had attacked her with a bunch of paint, finishes, and fixtures before getting her energy back in order. Imagine not bathing for years and then someone coming at you with a black dress and pearls and saying, "Here, put this on; you're going to feel great!" I think we can all agree that a clean dress and pearls even after one sweaty workout wouldn't feel great until we showered.

Based on this knowledge, I started making decisions on how I *felt* and the signs she would give me through my emotions. I would come to know this home as BoBo. It didn't take long to realize that I was developing a deep, meaningful relationship with her filled with love and respect. Together, we supported each other, nurtured each other, and fostered enormous positive growth. This is how I discovered the journey to a place called home. What I now call a person's Honey Haven.

It can be hard to swallow with a logical mind, but it bears repeating: your physical world affects your emotional world and vice versa. Your home is a third skin and should be treated like the family member she is. As a part of the family unit, it is your duty to care for her in the same way she cares for you and your family. And don't be surprised to see her acting out if you fail to keep up your side of the bargain. She mirrors your energy and reflects back to you what's showing up in your life. If you are ill, she's likely ill, too. Are you overly emotional lately? Look at her plumbing. Going through a big life change? Check her foundation or roof. Experiencing respiratory issues? Check the HVAC system. Concerned about your finances? May be time to look at your stove because it represents money. All of these things mirror your physical world and if you don't take care of her, trust me she will act out, and it will wreck havoc on your life.

MY PROMISE TO YOU

This book will teach you how to have a deep meaningful relationship with your home and your environment. It's going to take you beyond the rational mind, and down a spiritual journey that's filled with spiritual phenomena that lights you up and fills the voids. In *Living in a Mindful Universe*, authors Karen Newell and Dr. Eben Alexander share that,

> *"a spiritual hole in the core of one's being can't be filled with nonspiritual substance. That hole is un-fillable, except with "positive spiritual matter." Spiritual emptiness stems from a sense of isolation and separation, which is false, but devastating to the human who suffers it. Filling a void of spiritual emptiness with something in the physical world, like drugs, alcohol or sex may appear to ease the pain, but only temporarily."*

I bring this up because too often in our heavy, left analytical culture, we have been led to believe that we can *think* our way through anything. I know I did. However, the void you feel sends you down a disparate journey in the opposite direction of finding true peace, and without you realizing it you get lost in a sea of self-help books, addictions, bad behavior, materialism and toxic relationships AKA: clutter. If you disconnect from your home and see her as a separate entity, you'll lose a sense of self, feel detached, and will try to fill it with non-spiritual matter.

In order to have a meaningful relationship with your home and with yourself, you have to ditch logic and step into the world of energy and emotion. Only in this way can you establish how to truly connect with your home's energy, and see her as positive spiritual matter that feeds your soul.

COMING HOME

"We all have knowledge, but what we need is experience to transform it."
Mastin Kipp

$\mathcal{D}$ ecorating a home is certainly important. We can all agree that a beautiful space influences our mood and how we feel, but jumping into the process of decorating before getting the energy right is essentially putting lipstick on a pig. Whether your home is brand new, or 100 years old, it harbors energy. It may hold trauma, joy, bruises, happiness, sadness, humor, anger, and even war. Even if your home is brand new, you have to keep in mind two things: the land beneath your home is very old, and there were a lot of hands touching your home while she was being built. Those hands were having good days and having bad days. In addition, words and emotions were taking place every day, vibrating a frequency into her walls.

As an interior designer, I have spent many days on job sites. Contractors and trades are a colorful group of people. Some are the most delightful, kind, and knowledgeable people you'll ever meet.

Others feel that life is happening to them as opposed to for them, and they are the consummate victims just trying to survive the day. Early in my career, I can remember how exasperated these colorful people could make me feel. I think an interior designers greatest skill is being a solution-oriented ninja. Not only do we control and manage our portion of the job, but we often also find ourselves keeping everyone else on track as well, while simultaneously meeting the expectations of the client. Few contractors like having interior designers on the job, but it's often because of us that the job moves forward in a positive, beautiful, and productive way.

In 2005, right after my husband and I had moved to Nashville, I started working on a large Frank Lloyd Wright home about 50 miles South of downtown Nashville. It was a difficult job because it was filled with a bunch of good ol' boys who wanted to do things their way. In their eyes, I simply slowed things down. In my eyes, I was helping my client achieve a level of home she'd only dreamed of one day owning.

It was the day before Thanksgiving, and I was standing in the middle of a Publix grocery store trying to decide on ham or turkey when Barbara called me. "They don't have the tub, and they are installing the tile incorrectly. It's off-center but the tile guy won't listen to me! It's bad, it's all very bad!"

"Wait, slow down," I replied. "Why are they installing the tile today? I was told no one would be out there until Friday, and they can't install tile if they don't have the tub. They are putting the cart before the horse."

"Exactly!" Barbara shouted into the phone.

I paid for the small amount groceries I had managed to find and made the fifty mile trek to the job site. Sure enough, the tile guy was laying tile without a bathtub, estimating where he thought it should go, and laying it without symmetry or little regard for what the homeowner who was going to live there wanted. It looked terrible, and having just moved to Nashville from California, I couldn't believe how shoddy this all was.

Come to find out, the bath tub was supposed to be delivered the day before, but for some reason, the plumber never made it. Rather than figure out what happened to it and the plumber, the tile guy showed up and was "doing the job he was scheduled and paid to do."

I politely told him it doesn't work that way and that the tile would need to come down. Let's just say things got ugly. He didn't like being told by a woman he was doing a poor job. Angry, rude words were said, but Barbara and I were finally able to get him out of the house. After several phone calls I discovered that the plumber, who had the tub, had gone out for some drinks the night before he was supposed to deliver the tub, got in a bar fight, and ended up in jail. My client's bathtub was in a truck that had been impounded.

It was now late afternoon, the night before Thanksgiving, and there was nothing I could do about the tub. But I could see that this had rattled Barbara to the core. She was frustrated, disappointed, and I was afraid that this was going to ruin Thanksgiving with her family.

One of the first things necessary to start healing a home is mindset. Are you ready, willing, and able to heal your home? Are you ready to make her a part of the family and do whatever it takes to make her whole? Even when faced with lopsided, unsymmetrical tile? A clear mindset starts shifting the energy in the right direction because it sharpens your intent and tells that energy where to go and what you wish to experience. It's imperative to get the energy right to avoid falling into into the traps of negative soup that doesn't serve you. I call this Below the Cross Emotions, but more on that in a minute. What I have come to learn in my twenty plus years of practicing Feng Shui is that an intentional mindset alone changes everything, and I have my experience on this day with Barbara to thank for that.

Due to my abrupt departure from the grocery store, I didn't have any of my ceremonial tools. In the past, I would have seen those as necessary to move forward. I would have told myself that without them I wasn't effective. But without me realizing it, this was going to be a powerful lesson on mindset for us both.

I grabbed Barbara's hand and said, "Are you ready to get to work?" She looked me square in the eyes and without saying a word, she nodded yes.

For the next two hours, Barbara and I went to work on her home's energy. Without my tools, I felt like I was making it all up, flying by the seat of my pants, and doing what ever I could to make her feel better. But I quickly realized, just as BoBo had spoken to me through energy, Barbara's home was doing the same. She was guiding us in what she needed most, and that was love.

I was inspired to grab a Sharpie pen out of my car, and we wrote love notes to her home and placed them all over the house inside the walls. We both agreed that her home needed a name and we heard the word Frankie! She and I chanted mantras, we sang, and drew hearts and messages of love on the foundation, in the attic, and on the walls. There was an old plastic bucket that I turned into a drum, and as I pounded on it, Barbara sang her favorite gospels. Finally, we sat down on the dirty living room floor, grabbed each other's hands, and we prayed. I visualized that I had all the tools I needed, and that was the light of spirit and love. I asked that only love and peace surround this home, and I visualized a bubble of energy encapsulating the property and home. I asked that all negativity be eradicated and that moving forward only peace, love, and joy would remain.

I had no idea if I was doing a damn thing, but I visualized that my heart energy swelled in gratitude and surrounded Barbara and this beautiful home so they both could find peace. It would be years later that I would learn the true power of prayer, but I am forever grateful to Barbara and her home Frankie for teaching me that a positive mindset and positive intent are all it takes to start healing a home's energy, even if it looks like a scene straight from Woodstock!

WHAT IS A HEALTHY HOME?

Creating a healthy home can seem like a huge undertaking, but trust me when I say, it's one well worth taking. Many people want to skip straight to the pretty part, and they view the energy part as either pure nonsense or a journey not worth taking. I mean, does it *really* matter? Since your home is a direct reflection of you and your family, a healthy home is necessary to live a healthy and fulfilled life. So yeah, it does matter. Not only should great care go into the way you care for her mechanics and systems, but also the way you care for her energy and beauty. Cheap carpet, bargain paints, low-priced mattresses, discounted furniture, low cost lighting, competitive cleaners, and budget-friendly accessories are no way to fill a home with love. And neither are cheap building products. It's essentially like feeding your kids McDonalds every day for breakfast, lunch, and dinner and not expecting any repercussions. Many would argue that they don't have a choice because they have a budget. Guess what? You always have a choice, and it starts with planning rather than buying in hurried haste. Trust me, I've been an interior designer for just as long as I've been a Feng Shui practitioner, and there is always a way to buy more intentionally. And good design with positive intent takes time to curate.

Many of the products we fill our homes with today are filled with enormous amounts of toxins that stress our energetic systems to the point of severe illness. Headaches, fatigue, asthma, indigestion, skin ailments, infertility and more can all be traced back to the chemicals we are doused in every day. Comet, one of the least expensive cleaners on the market, has been proven to emit 146 different chemicals into the air when used, which has been linked to cancer, asthma, and reproductive disorders. The biggest offenders being formaldehyde, benzene, chloroform, and toluene, which are not listed on the label. Continuing the use of such practices also harms your home's energy. If you are ill and experiencing any of the aforementioned symptoms like headaches or severe fatigue, this affects how you care for your home. It also affects the vibration you emit and deposit within your home. Everything is a holistic cobweb of energy frequency bouncing around your home, and it either contributes to raising vibrations or lowers it. Your environment either supports you or it doesn't; it's never neutral. And the decisions you make every day affect that energy.

When a home is sick, dilapidated, and worn down, so are you. You'll find yourself sick often, not feeling well and depressed. A home that looks weak feels weak. Have you ever gone into a space that was dark and cluttered and you just couldn't breathe? Or you suddenly get tired and fatigued? This is not a supportive environment. It will influence your decisions and, before you know, it you're making poor food decisions, avoiding the gym, and making poor life choices. The energy literally drags you down and depletes you. On the flip side, a healthy home is strong and vibrant, making you feel like you can take on the world. Either way, both have the power to influence your mood, so which do you want to cultivate?

Everything is energy and holds energy. Cut corners and hold the wrong mindset and that will carry forward in your home's energy, and yours, like an unrewarding time stamp. Physicists discovered more than a century ago and proved that physical atoms are made up of energy vortices that are constantly spinning and vibrating, creating a unique energy blueprint. In Feng Shui, we call this *Chi*, or energy. All of us are beings of energy and vibration, radiating a unique energy signature, and that even includes the hard surfaces in your home. In fact, matter isn't solid at all, but its vibration is so slow it appears to be!

This revelation that the universe is not a collection of seemingly hard physical parts but rather a holistic cobweb of vibrational energy frequencies stems from the early works of Albert Einstein, and many other turn-of-the-century scientists. In spite of quantum physicists proving that matter is nothing but an illusion, the very idea that it might be true is still greeted with cynicism and even superstition.

So where does that leave us in creating a healthy home? Well, if our physical world isn't physical at all, how can we explore the efficacy of this further? How can we make it better? That's simple: by better understanding energy.

The challenge with this concept, what I call the "woo," is that many in mainstream thought remain within the boundaries of only that which can be perceived in our analytical and logical mind. But is it possible to think our way through this? Nope. Keep in mind that our visual spectrum compared to what's actually available is very limited. So, not only can you not think your way through this, you'll likely not see your way through it either. The only way you'll experience it, is to *feel* your way through it. A skillset that I can honestly say is one that needs to be honed and developed because most of our population has been shamed and guilted out of feeling anything. To do otherwise is to show weakness, so stop being so emotional!

I think it's safe to say that our minds, no matter how many materialist scientists want to say it's false, do not create consciousness. Our minds filter it from the Universe, and that's what creates our reality. As RC Henry was quoted saying in The Mental Universe,

> *The Mind no longer appears to be an accidental intruder into the realm of matter, rather, it is the creator and governor of the realm of manifestation.*

In other words, the things you surround yourself with, including your home and even your old duct-taped beanbag, are manifested reality via your energy consciousness.

In order to create a healthy home, you've gotta go beyond logic and reason. You have to see this through a spiritual lens that's antithetical to every logical thing you've ever learned about your so-called reality. Every decision counts—your thoughts, your actions—it all matters, because it's all energy. You've gotta become the creator that manifests love and positive spiritual matter within your home because she is far more than the layout, pretty paint and decorations. Through her, if you get the energy right, you'll return to a place and see it for the first time; that place is you—the almighty, magnificent you.

Since everything is energy and holds energy, it can be easy to get caught up in a negative loop pattern. Many people default to negative emotions as a badge of honor. Problem is, when energy gets stuck and stagnant, negative energy pockets can arise and pull you into energy tornados that can seem confusing. In an instant, your mood shifts and you're pissed off or sad, and you have no idea why you're having this sweep of unexpected emotions. You're not crazy; you just plugged into an old pattern left behind from countless episodes of negativity. This has become your manifested reality. Before you know it, a decade goes by and the energy is so thick it can be hard to breathe.

A healthy home changes everything. It makes you come alive, it shifts the family dynamic and shifts the energy in everything it touches. Through love and care, you can change your holistic cobweb of vibrational energy into one that is full of balanced, harmonious Chi, better known as a healthy home.

Making small changes every day to create a healthy home transforms, transmutes, and transcends those old energy patterns, pushing you forward into new opportunities and circumstances that make life incredible. And this is something you *feel*. A healthy home matters because it eliminates headaches, anxiety, and frustration. All you have to do is make smart choices every day, mindfully, to help your home become and stay healthy. Moreover, you'll become healthy, too. Hot damn!

Creating a healthy home is fairly simple; it's one that is free of as many toxins as possible, and that includes a toxic mindset. I can attest that with good energy comes great beauty and happiness within a home. A healthy home allows her beauty and energy to shine through. It's full of nutritious organic foods, has no harsh cleaning chemicals, and few off-gassing products. Words and thoughts are kind, and care is brought forth in everything that enters and exits the home. Sustainable practices are in place, and with all of that, great beauty will follow. As I always say, beautiful energy is what equals a beautiful home because it's rooted in love.

HONEY HEART BLESSINGS

Just like you your home is a living entity of vibrational energy vortices, a home that is filled with toxins and tons of clutter (bad behavior, toxic relationships, lousy habits, unhealthy mindsets along with unwanted stuff) is an occupant filled with negative Chi. Toxic thinking, toxic relationships, and a toxic environment are the energetic, clutter trifecta of anxiety, lack of clarity, chaos and illness. Unfortunately, this represents the average American home because to see their home as anything beyond physical matter is typically met with pessimism.

So why do you want to step outside of logic and into the world of feeling? Your environment influences your mood. How you think, how you behave, and the decisions you make are a direct result of your energy environment. Awareness is key in order to heal you and your home. Not to mention, tapping into your emotional, energetic states are your direct line to God. In other words, your intuition. If your current circumstances are good, and everything is going the way that you want it to go, great! You're likely not in need of this book. Send the good Chi forward and donate it. But for the rest of you looking to heal yourself and your home, in order to eliminate the negative Chi, it's going to require less doubt and more heart-centered feeling work. This is how you create your own Woodstock!

When a homeowner enters a space with excitement, motivation, and love, she is ready to take on anything. This is how I felt when I met my California house, BoBo. I was ready to take on the world in an effort to heal her. I was ready, willing, and able to do whatever it took to make her whole again, even if that meant I had to look crazy according to mainstream thought. "Why yes, I am experiencing panic attacks because my house can't breathe. How do I know? Oh, she told me so." Sarcasm aside, I cared for her as the family member she was. And she felt my excitement, my eagerness to make it right again. Together, we healed one another. I cared for her and I loved on her hard, and she did the same for me. This is what I call a Honey Heart. Creating positive spiritual matter through the energy of unconditional love via your home.

A Honey Heart is willing to do what ever it takes to the best of her ability to remove toxins, unnecessary stress, and all negativity, and replace it with positive practices that have meaning to her and her relationship to her home. By doing this, she creates a sacred space that goes far beyond the four walls that most would call home. This space supports her in every way possible, uplifts her, encourages her, and heals her hurts so that she and her family can live their best life. She understands that only when beautiful energy is combined with beautiful things can you attain a beautiful home and life.

A HONEY HEART IN THE MAKING

On that cold November day, unbeknownst to her, Barbara was a Honey Heart in the making. On this day, she and her home became the best of friends. The energy that we had created, and the love that we built was palpable. We were able to remove the traumas, bruises, and sadness, and uplift both of them to a level that I would argue was beyond what Barbara had ever felt. It was also an incredible lesson in the power of energy work, intent, and what you can accomplish when you put your mind to it.

It's been many years since that fateful day of a missing bath tub, but this is what I know for sure after years of study, teachers and mentors: we are powerful, omniscient beings if we set our minds to something. It's also a true testament to the power of prayer. I was once told by a mentor that if we, as earthly beings, understood who walks beside us we'd never hold an inkling of doubt or fear.

Additionally, it showed the power of the collective mind. When Barbara and I came together that day, we didn't question logic or fear of looking crazy, albeit, we probably looked nuts, but we knew what we had to do to change and shift the energy. We instinctively knew that if we didn't come together, we'd continue down a long dark negative path that would be arduous and grueling.

COMING TO A PLACE CALLED HOME

When we left Barbara's house, it was dark and had started to rain. Despite how the day had started, and in spite of the encroaching colder weather, Barbara had a light in her eyes again. Her energy had shifted, and I could feel her joy. The impulse to 'get to work' on the energy had paid off. Even though it seemed nuts to move forward without any real direction, Frankie knew exactly what we needed to do. We threw logic to the wayside and *felt* our way through impulse and delirious intuition. It was incredibly fun!

When I got home that night, I never shared with my family what really happened that day in the woods, south of Nashville. It seemed too sacred to get questioned or laughed at. The last thing I needed was sarcasm and cynicism when this day held so much beauty. That day, those woods were our church. I knew that there was no way I could explain or justify what I had felt, or what I had experienced. The incident with the tub and plumber was a far more logical resource to tell my family why I ditched the grocery store and failed to get Thanksgiving dinner.

I tried to reason with my own sanity, so I told myself that while it felt like an initiation into something greater, I did it to make Barbara feel better. See what I did there? I pushed feeling aside and tried to think my way through it, but as we well know, energy doesn't work that way. And energy is our connection and communication to the divine. Learn to listen. I could feel the stirring in my soul. I knew I was on to something different, even though I didn't know exactly what that was. And like Barbara, I too was becoming a Honey Heart, but in a much different way.

WELCOME TO THE HAVEN

When a home is truly cared for and loved as the family member she is, it creates a happy, supportive environment where everyone thrives. This is what I call a Honey Haven. A healing space that becomes sacred and uplifting that can't be felt in the outside world, but you carry it with you. This space, this atmosphere, changes everyone's mood that inhabits it, that comes in contact with it or catches a glimpse of it. It's like walking into a vortex of healing, positive energy. Many people who come in contact with *it* say it's like feeling a warm hug. It's a sense that you are safe and welcome. Here, you are completely cared for. But bear in mind, this cannot be achieved solely through decoration. Only through her energy and your love can you create a happy, healthy home.

With that said, not everyone can accomplish this. Despite your best efforts, you may try and fall flat. You say to yourself, *well I've set my mind to it and I have the intent, why isn't this working, Amanda? Why doesn't my home feel like a warm hug? Why can't I tap into that feeling that you and Barbara had that day in the woods? I wanna get weird too!* In most American homes, anything beyond the physical that lies outside the visual spectrum is met with cynicism and pessimism. If your Chi holds fear or doubt it's going to be impossible to rise above to the good stuff. Only through what I call *Above the Cross Emotions* will you be able to touch the magic and explore the extraordinary, unexplainable phenomenon that steeps your soul and allows you to come head to head with your own Woodstock moment.

ABOVE AND BELOW THE CROSS EMOTIONS

When joy, happiness and good health envelopes a home, negative energy like doubt, frustration, anger, and worry cannot survive. It's impossible for them to commingle because, on a vibrational level, they don't match. It's essentially like two opposing magnets. Unfortunately, most people are swimming in a sea of doubt, fear, frustration, and anger all the time.

Your thoughts, emotions, and words all have a vibrational power. You are the creator of your own destiny, and thoughts are the first step to manifestation and what shows up in your environment. In fact, thoughts precede physical manifestation. According to Psychology Today, humans have between 12,000 to 60,000 thoughts per day, and as many as 98 percent are exactly the same thoughts you had the day before. Even more significant and alarming, is that 80 percent of those thoughts are negative. Most people's thoughts are so scattered and on the wrong frequency, their reality ends up not amounting to much. Remember, these are the same thoughts and vibrational emotions you repeat and deposit inside your home.

Thinking perpetual negative thoughts is what I refer to as *Below the Cross Emotions.* Under stress, your brain frequency speeds up and causes you to get caught up in a negative loop. This causes you to be scattered and frenetic and affects your immune system because, in this state of anxiety, frustration, and fear, your nervous system is always on alert. Scientists call this incoherence, where the heart and brain communicate in a trivial, erratic way that manifests as stress.

This state also radically affects the things that manifest around you. If you are constantly swimming in fear, doubt, shame, guilt, anger, and judgmental thinking, it's nearly impossible to attract happiness, joy, and peace. The vibrations don't match. You may be able to temporarily grasp the good stuff but you won't be able to hang onto it unless you're willing to become it.

"You cannot have what you're not willing to become vibrationally. If you do get it, you'll lose it—that's why people who win the lottery lose it. Or they get the person they think they want to be with but they can't keep the relationship. Or they get a modicum of success but can't hold onto it because inside they weren't vibrationally aligned to it, they hadn't become it. So you can temporarily manipulate and get things but to have it completely you have to lift your vibration and when you are at the vibration you're no longer attracting it, you're radiating the manifestation."

Dr. Michael Beckwith

We often use words to label and express our feeling energy. But when feeling, expressing, and speaking words, they all carry with them a vibrational frequency that goes out into the ether, and more often than not, the words used aren't positive. Many are self-loathing, undeserving, hateful, judgmental, and self-deprecating. In order to become the vibration of what you desire most, you have to do every-thing you can to break the loop of negative thinking and negative speaking.

For over 20 years, Dr. David Hawkins studied *The Map of Consciousness* via a process called muscle testing. His research revealed seventeen stages of consciousness, and the goal was to assist in human evolution by raising people's awareness on what was possible through their states of emotions. You can learn more through his book, *Power Versus Force* and *Transcending the Levels of Consciousness*. According to his work, 78% of the population is in negative soup, based on their level of consciousness. What exactly is consciousness? In my opinion, it's the filter we place on reality. All you have to do is go out in public for a few hours and see that the reality each of us holds is very different. And honestly, quite negative.

According to his human Richter scale, our biggest shift occurs when we hit courage. This is the stage of integrity and where we can start discerning truth from falsehoods by ascending the ego mind. This reality starts the climb out of negative soup and helps us see the bigger picture, albeit here we are still wearing smudged glasses.

As we ascend, we enter into the higher map of consciousness states, which is what I call *Above the Cross Emotions*. Here we find gratitude, pleasure, happiness, and love. When you can rise above anger and fear, you reach a state of courage and can see the world as exciting and full of possibility. Life starts to feel manageable and, where a gap exists, you attain a growth mindset that acts to fill it through positive means, like learning new things. Rather than attaining more stuff in life, you choose growth through wisdom. You acquire less and savor more and, rather than maintaining the same old patterns, you find new ways to evolve. Pleasure and satisfaction come from within rather than without and life starts to become transcendent. Now, instead of radiating fear and worry within the walls of your home, you're transmitting love and joy. Can you *feel* the difference this might hold within a space?

This is how you radiate the manifestation as opposed to attracting it momentarily. This is a pivotal shift in you and how you cultivate personal Chi to achieve a constant state of feeling *Above the Cross Emotions*. When you can achieve this state of awareness, your reality begins to shift. Your mindset is open and your intention becomes crystal clear. This is how you can touch the magic and explore extraordinary, unexplainable phenomenon that embraces and fills your soul. Because only in this state will you be able to achieve extraordinary Feng Shui results and understand energy in a way you never thought possible. Welcome Home!

2

WHAT THE FENG SHUI

"Doors will open where there were no doors before, where you would not have thought there were going to be doors and where there wouldn't be a door for anybody else."
Joseph Campbell

*a*fter that day at the bookstore, I felt alive again. I finally had pinpointed the reason for my panic attacks, and I felt empowered knowing how to fix it. For the first time since we bought the house, I demanded that the contractor get the front door operational. No more excuses or putting us off. His crew showed up the next morning at 6 AM. Before I knew it, I was in the field next door, trying to scoop up my cat Nike that Wayne the foreman had let out. I didn't care. I looked Wayne square in the eyes and told him I wanted temporary stairs built up to the front of the house and some sort of an operational door—and I wanted it done today. Panic attacks no more!

Wayne, of course, thought I was nuts, but I didn't care. At the time, I had been working at an outpatient surgery center and had to get to work by 6:30AM. When I got home later that afternoon, I could not believe how much better I felt. Even if it was a temporary door situation, it made all the difference. I could sense BoBo's breath; her Chi was breathing and the entire air within and around the home felt different. It was what would become my first of many spiritual experiences.

It wasn't long after this experience that a friend and I were having lunch, and she suggested I look up the woman from the bookstore, Marlene. I had absolutely no idea how to find her. You have to remember that this was back in the 90's. Some people had Internet, but I was not one of them. And even if I did have it, I wouldn't have had a clue how to use it. Some may argue that I still don't know how to use it. Back then, very few people or businesses were on the web. You could argue that it was a few geeks and maybe Amazon.

As luck would have it, I was at a metaphysic book shop about a month later looking for more "F" word books. Once again, I was totally out of my element. It smelled funny, and there were weird sculptures of fat guys, scary dragons, esoteric books about witches, dream catchers, and sparkly things hanging everywhere. Anti-hermetic music was playing in the background that sounded like a man being stabbed to death. There were funny tie-dyed curtains hanging along the wall and brightly colored, shiny rocks everywhere, mixed with angels, occult cards, and what looked to be voodoo tools. The people peppered throughout the space were a motley crew. It included an old woman with long grey hair in a caftan, a goth chick with black lipstick, and a middle-aged man in slacks who looked so uncomfortable but desperate for help.

As I perused the books, a woman emerged from one of the tie-dyed curtains. It was Marlene! I couldn't believe my luck. When our eyes met, I must have looked like an excited three-year old about to get ice cream. She giggled and waved, then walked over.

"Have we met?" she asked.

"As a matter of fact we have. It was because of you, I started learning about Feng Shui. Remember Borders bookstore?" I said.

"Oh yes! Yes that's right!" she said clapping her hands together with yet another famous big smile.

I couldn't place my finger on it but this woman radiated light. There was a twinkle in her eye and a resonance with her that I had never experienced. I would later learn after many, many soul books like those written by by Dr. Brian Weiss, and Dr. Micheal Newton, and countless others that this was soul recognition.

She grabbed my arm and said, "Let's sit and chat."

Before I knew it, she was asking me about my deceased Aunt.

"Oh, who's Susie?" She screeched!

"Ummm, Susie? Uh, she was my aunt." I said, baffled and confused.

"Oh darling she's so proud of you, so proud. But medicine isn't for you, love. Nope. You have another calling. This thing you're doing isn't your purpose. You are being pulled in another direction, another calling. Is there something else you want to do?" she asked bright eyed with excitement.

Still taken aback by this whirlwind of information I stuttered, "Umm, I mean, I'm not really sure."

"Oh, but you do!" She laughed out loud. "It's Feng Shui!"

"Wait, what? I'm supposed to do *that*?" I managed to blurt out.

"She's working her magic; she's showing you the way. Pay attention and listen. Those doors are closing," she said with all seriousness.

"Who's working her magic?" I said with confusion. "Susie?"

"No, no, no." She chuckled out loud. "Spirit, my love. Spirit!"

Good grief, I thought, *that was weird!*

As I drove home from that bookstore, I was a mix of emotions, excited by the possibility, and also terrified. I was trying to go over in my head how I was going to tell my mother that I was ditching med school for this weird esoteric thing that I knew she'd never heard of called Feng Shui. Better yet, my very non-woo, left-brain husband. Simultaneously, I was excited because I had never felt THIS way about medicine—yet another energy clue that you're on the right path versus the wrong one.

What I find interesting about energy is that, when you tap into it and honor it, work with it and sit with it, life will open up for you in unimaginable ways. After countless interviews over the years about how I got into Feng Shui, the one thing everyone is always most fascinated about is how I knew my purpose. How I could ditch a prominent profession like medicine for something I knew nothing about based solely on a feeling. I think many could call this blind faith. But inquisitive minds are curious about this thing called purpose and feel they lack the knowing path, when in actuality we've all felt it, we just choose to ignore it because the "what-ifs" and the "when I do this, then that can happen" gets in the way.

When I got home that night, I kept my mouth shut. I had to get my wits about me and figure out how the hell I was going to break the big news. But I needed to have a plan! How on Earth do you study Feng Shui? In ancient times, children went on a vision quest to be gifted the vision of their purpose. Once they were gifted their purpose, an elder would take them under their wing and train them. In the Andes, before the conquistadors and the Catholic Church rose to power, the Laika wisdom keepers had mystery schools to learn and teach their gifts. With neither of these in place today, I had to figure out how on Earth I was going to learn this esoteric thing called Feng Shui. What I knew for sure was that I would need the ability to get into homes. I narrowed it down to two professions, either real estate or interior design.

I knew nothing about either profession. But once again, Miss Spirit took the lead. Just as Marlene had told me, spirit was guiding me. The very next day, I opened up the newspaper—yes the newspaper—and there was a small ad for a special design school in town. It was a small boutique school that specialized in creative arts. Very much like a mystery school, this design education would be taught orally and hands-on by other professionals in the same field. This sounded amazing! They only accepted 30 students a year for each creative program, and they would be opening enrollment for their design program in three weeks. When I saw the ad, a flurry of butterflies swooped into my stomach and rushed out the top of my head. I knew right away that this was Spirit speaking to me. Or maybe it was BoBo; either way, I was listening! But then logic stepped in. Why on Earth would they accept a med student with a degree in biology? I had no business in a creative field!

Energy is a funny thing. If you flow with her, honor her, and allow her the sacred space to evolve within you, she'll show you the way. If you ignore her and disrespect her with hasty opinion, she can make life challenging and downright miserable. Over the course of the next three weeks, I went on a roller coaster of yes/no hyperbole, swinging from one extreme to the next. But I kept it to myself. I had devised a plan to apply to the school and only if I got accepted would I break it to my family. Why set off unnecessary land mines if I didn't need to? But I should give credit where credit is due. My mama knew something was up. She had seen me doing weird things around the house, and talking about this energy stuff, and like a clever fox, her mama instincts knew something was up. So I told her about the school and that I was applying. To my surprise she was relieved.

"You don't belong in medicine," she very calmly stated. Very matter of factly, she followed with, "You've been a weird, creative child your whole life."

"Umm, thanks mom?"

When I went through the interview process, I never felt more like a fish out of water. Everyone was so pretty and well-dressed and oozing creativity. Their hair was perfectly coifed, and everyone had that cool creative vibe to them, and here I was the dorky science student. In the medical world, everything was always stoic and professional, analytical and competitive. These people were different. When I went into my interview, I immediately went into "professional upstanding citizen, I'm super smart person" mode. I was here to impress them, right? Well, I was not prepared for the first question.

"What makes you really come alive and what do most hope to feel from it?"

Ummm, what in the what? How do I want to feel? Oh dear lord, I've landed in the middle of Alien Gypsies. I remember nothing after the first question. In fact, I don't even remember walking to my car, but speaking of feelings, I felt deflated and very uncool. I knew I had bombed that interview, and my dream of being creative and weird professionally was history. Who needed Feng Shui anyways?

WHAT THE FENG SHUI!

In the simplest of terms, when I am asked what Feng Shui is, my response is always the same. It is a tool to help you increase flow and abundance in all areas of your life through one of the safest prescriptions on the planet, energy medicine. It shows you how we mortal humans can harmonize with this thing called Chi, or energy, the vital cosmic breath of all creation. In more complex terms, it shows you how to unite with the compassionate collective mind, take skillful action, and trust in a process that links man to the universe through Tao. Translated as the way or the path, Tao reflects the purest way to tap into the everlasting rhythms of life to achieve equilibrium, or the yin and yang of life, which we will discuss further in Chapter 3.

For many in the modern world, the term Feng Shui addresses practical solutions on where to place your desk or perhaps your bed, and how to manage your physical clutter. However, Feng Shui can also be used on a grander scale. It can encompass the shape of your home or your lot, integrate a community, or embrace entire urban planning. Taking energy, or Chi, into consideration is what creates balance and complete energy alignment in whatever you are assessing. Beyond its practical nature and benefits, Feng Shui is an intuitive, practical science that seeks to teach you how to develop a positive relationship with your environment. One that supports you rather than depletes you. By combining ancient wisdom with modern knowledge, we can build highly suitable conditions for optimal living.

As mentioned in the previous chapter, even though much of Feng Shui cannot be seen, it can be felt. It brings an awareness to your home beyond the visual spectrum. It looks at her shape, layout, orientation, and her surroundings and takes into account that if these elements, any of them, are unfavorable, it can affect your routines, activities, moods, and overall health, and disrupt finances and relationships. In spite of many seeing Feng Shui as a mere superstition, unable to explain how these elements can possibly disrupt so much in our lives, ultimately it promotes happiness and success by making adjustments that strengthen Chi to benefit you in every way possible.

What attracted me to The Black Sect Feng Shui tradition was its ability to combine long-established knowledge with the intangible or non-physical, and it also places great importance on intention. To me, this is soul work disguised as playing with energy to improve your house. Utilizing your own Chi to manipulate your energy environment not only bridges you from the external world to your internal world but also creates a potent force of empowerment. You come face to face with this thing called inner wisdom and universal intelligence. Rather than looking to extraneous chattels like decorations as a source to fix your environment, Feng Shui gives you the ability to create your own suitable environment for your needs. This is both a science and an art, learning how to communicate between the Chi of your environment and your own. Rather than focusing on tools like directions or compass theory as a way of interpreting space, your greatest tool comes from understanding Chi flow and understanding yourself. How Chi enters a space, where it comes from, and how it meanders throughout will all be interpreted through understanding your intuition.

SHUI WORK IS SOUL WORK

According to Energy expert Donna Eden, energy is the gateway to optimal health, vitality and joy. In her book, Energy Medicine, she writes:

> *You are a latticework of energies. The enormous implications of this single fact are the basis of energy medicine. I invite you to step into a domain that exists beyond the world of appearances and explore how invisible energies shape the way you feel, the way you think and the way you live.*

Throughout this book, I will be sharing not only stories of my own, but those of my friends and clients to help you on your Feng Shui journey. These stories will go beyond reason and logic and likely threaten existing beliefs that you've carried your entire life. Maybe not; some of us were lucky enough to be raised by open minded, wild, and free hippies. (Cheers to you mama!) However, most were not. And those beliefs can hold you back in a tragic loop of forever revolving negativity rather than rising to your greatest evolution.

What if I told you everything could change? That you hold the key, the very power within you to ignite all the tools you need to have the life you've always dreamed of? You do! I encourage you to lean in to the idea that energy is the key to better health and well-being, and it's time you start dancing with the unseen forces around you to optimize your body's natural capacities and your environment's ability to help you heal. Through a strong healthy body filled with vibrant Chi, you simultaneously create an environment that matches your stamina. By elevating both, you can reduce stress and anxiety, free yourself from worry, and improve every area of your life—all with this little tool called Feng Shui. Furthermore, you'll be able to take what you learn and not only apply it to yourself but apply what you learn to benefit your friends and family as well. What modern profit-centered health-care system can say that in their marketing?

To me, Shui work is Soul Work. Over the years, I've been asked what the benefits of Feng Shui are and why people should do it. I think one of the best examples is that it's safe, natural, and accessible to anyone who is willing to try it. One such example is the almighty power of the front door, which I briefly talked about in the introduction. Known as the mouth of Chi in Feng Shui, the front door is energy medicine for your entire home. This seemingly mundane feature goes from being just the entrance of your home to the great grandmother that nourishes every part of your life. Fail to care for this energy and your life will suffer.

While at an energy workshop at Kripalu in the Berkshires of Massachusetts last fall, I learned of a student who complained of job loss, lack of opportunity, not being able to breathe... Uh, sound familiar? She was literally describing the exact experience I had while living in my California house, BoBo. She had attended this workshop to learn how to clear the energy out of her home to start getting things right again. Problem is, no amount of energy clearing will fix a mouth that's been wired shut.

During a break out session, I had my chance to find out more. Laura, an energy practitioner, had won a 10' x 10' infrared sauna. How exciting, right? Well, that is until I realized that the only place she could put said sauna was in her entryway. As she put it, "The house has really small rooms full of furniture. The entry was the one space it fit, and I wasn't using the front door anyway."

Not only had she placed the sauna in the entryway, she had hired a contractor to seal it into place! Ack! What's worse is the sauna broke a year later! Now she couldn't use her front door, and the thing blocking her front door was broken. This is where you have to tap into your energy strengths and trust the intelligence of your intuition. Your environment speaks to you. Listen to what it's telling you. Ignoring those clues is a very harmful way to practice energy. Unlike me who knew nothing about energy at the time, Laura was well versed in energy. Fortunately, it's easier than you think to update your energy software and adapt to this new way of looking at your environment. You'll learn all this throughout this book, but first, rip out the broken sauna or any other things blocking your front door!

I think what's most exciting about the increasing popularity in people's interest in ancient wisdom right now is this return to personal authority and empowerment, a return to our ancestors and how they taught us to harmonize with the forces of nature that feed our body, mind, and soul. Regardless of the bright, shiny object syndrome you hold for modern day technologies, the essence of ancient wisdom around energy still holds true. Despite a new iPhone being launched every six months, energy doesn't change. After millennia, the only thing that has changed is our ability to interpret energy through our senses, which have been mutilated by trivial distractions and modern day conveniences that are nothing short of illusion.

Another incredible benefit to working with energy and Feng Shui is that it's an inside job, literally. By taking the time to cultivate your energy, your Chi, and that of your environment, you become the wise healer. You gain empowerment to overcome your personal obstacles and challenges rather than seeking external help that may come at you with a one-size-fits-all approach. As Anthony Stevens states,

"Beneath our conscious intelligence a deeper intelligence is at work - the evolved intelligence of humankind."

In ancient times, theologians would have initiates study the vastness of the night sky to help them understand the vastness of the soul within them. This is how they could grasp the idea of the power, the energy within them. In spite of the fact that many scientists state that consciousness dies when we do, the materialist point of view that I spoke of in Chapter 1, a new way of quantum physics is proving otherwise through a concept called filter theory. Instead of producing consciousness, the brain is seen to filter consciousness, and who we are is an expression of that essence. This is our soul essence. The soul is the source of all subtle energy that surrounds us; even the tree outside your window has soul essence. Understanding your energy is to understand your soul, and to understand the soul is a peek into understanding the universe. So, if Spirit is the omnipotent intelligent energy of all creation, the soul is a piece of that manifestation. A great example of this is taking a bucket of water from the ocean. The ocean could be seen as the universe and the bucket of water could be seen as you, the extension of the Universe.

So, how is this a benefit of Feng Shui? How can we see Shui work as soul work? Soul and Spirit are one and the same. They are unfathomable, creating the vital unexplained mysteries of our very energetic existence. Through our environment, loved ones, friends, and even the stranger at the store, we experience the magic of soul energy every day through love, joy, happiness, and other emotion.

"Einstein proved through physics what the sages have taught for thousands of years: everything in our material world - animate and inanimate - is made of energy and everything radiates energy. The continuously unfolding and dynamic nature of the Universe can only be understood as the work of a higher guiding intelligence of another dimension."
William Collinge

Bottom line, energy work is soul work. Every day you do Feng

Shui, you tap into the divine, that higher intelligence. The soul is your drop of the ocean within you that animates your body and creates your reality with the collective mind. To work with a person's energy and their environment is to touch their soul. And the deeper you go, the more you'll enter a deeper level of your soul that is from the core of universal intelligence. When these energies are brought together in a skillful way, your body and environment will flourish, and your ocean can make waves in the world. This is the reason to do Feng Shui. To prepare and show your soul how to be nurtured and supported through our existence in this physical world.

YOUR JOURNEY INTO HEALING

For years I've been asked by folks who want to experiment with their own healing, "But, how exactly do I do this?"

It never ceases to amaze me, when I tell a story like the one of me and Barbara getting weird out in the woods, how quickly we can overthink and overcomplicate it. And let's not forget, in the moment I too almost allowed logic to get in the way. The good news is, the nature of energy medicine is changing, in that it's becoming more widely accepted. The bad news is our comfort level to practice it isn't. Soon, however, we will come to know ourselves and our environments as multi-sensory energetic entities that we have the power to manipulate. Through knowledge, experimentation, and experience, we will move beyond speculation about whether our thoughts and emotions have creative authority and see it as fact. Professor Lin was often quoted as saying, "Today's science fiction is tomorrow's fact."

When you can reach the point of acceptance—that you are more powerful than you know—and that this is the central truth of life, you'll achieve more contentment and healing than you've ever known.

"The day science begins to study non-physical phenomena, it will make more progress in one decade than in all the previous centuries of its existence."
Nikola Tesla

Repressing energy, treating it poorly, and ignoring it will soon become an obsolete way of thinking and will instead be replaced with beneficial healing modalities like Feng Shui to mend it. There is a rise in holistic therapies and growing interest in people wanting to create healthy home environments. The way we've been operating is no longer serving us or supporting us. Research has shown that our environments impact our thoughts and emotion, not to mention our overall health. The results from research are clear: the body, mind, spirit connection has to be honored as a whole system to produce an accurate portrait of health and well-being.

When we look around at the state of our healthcare, planet, politics, and even culture, it seems unwise to not acknowledge that we have lost our mind, body, spirit connection. There is a void, a disconnect. We are searching for that spiritual matter to fill the holes with alcohol, sex, shopping, food, and other addictions. Our energy has literally become frantic and incoherent due to stress, and we are driving it into the wrong things. But if we pay attention, energetics will be the thread to help us reshape our world. It will be the medicine that plugs us back in and turns us on to evolve into the spiritual beings we are meant to be.

When it comes to your own journey of healing, know that your greatest weapon and sharpest tool is you. You are the one who inhabits the space, and the body that needs healing. You have the ability to optimize your natural abilities by slowing down and tuning in. You'll achieve this by learning how to cultivate your Chi, which you'll learn in this book. In cultivating your abilities, you'll learn a language that you already know. It's the language of energy; you've just forgotten how to speak it. We've become so alienated from the natural order, buried in our phones and other distractions, that we've forgotten how to live in conscious partnership with our energy. But it is only through this language that you'll be able to live fully. You have to remember your software was designed for living in the wild, not confined within cars, high rises, and cubicles.

Nonetheless, you harbor one of the greatest gifts you've ever owned and have likely underestimated its value: your energy. This intelligence not only animates your Chi, but each and every cell emits and responds to electrochemical signals in your environment. In order to meaningfully engage the soul, however, and tap into that higher intelligence, you must turn to your heart. Yep, you guessed it, you have to *feel* your way into healing. This is how you can speak the language of home. Interestingly, after reading *Living in a Mindful Universe* by Dr. Eben Alexander and Karen Newell, I learned that, due to its shape, our heart's electrical field is sixty times greater than the brain, but its magnetic field is five thousand times greater than the brain. And here we put so much emphasis in our modern world on logic as opposed to emotion and feeling. No wonder so many people are running on operating systems with mental illness, chronic disease, and addiction.

The problem with this rational model is it has led us down a path of striving and surviving. The personification of the "haves and the have nots." In an effort to suppress emotions like fear, worry, and doubt rather than looking to the spiritual matter or energy medicine, we've looked to the acquisition of money, power, status, beauty, and other external things to heal us. Unfortunately, most come up empty. We have been led to believe that, in order to solve our problems, we must seek to change our outward circumstances rather than sharpen our inner assets.

Feng Shui is designed to give you tools to heal you and your environment. It is your natural ability to fix, heal, and maintain the energy around you that will be your most remarkable feats. You've been placed in a world that systematically interferes with your belief systems and natural capacity to heal, making you feel powerless and perhaps hopeless. You are so much more than you've been led to believe. Through conscious involvement, you will not only be empowered, but by learning these tools, you will truly prosper in all areas of your life. Our health and wellness need not be difficult or expensive, despite what we've been told. Furthermore, the suggestions given throughout this book are simple and effective, and many are free.

YOU LIKE ME, YOU REALLY LIKE ME

On the drive home after my interview at the boutique creative arts school, not only was I convinced that Feng Shui would never see the light of day as a career choice, I had also talked myself out of ever wanting to do it professionally. *What a stupid pipe dream,* I thought. Despite my logic playing tennis with reason, the truth was, my heart was broken. But I refused to *feel* it. It wasn't a worthy enough emotion to acknowledge, because it was silly of me to think that a science geek like me would ever be accepted into a cool, creative school. Side note: every emotion deserves to be felt, processed, and honored. Suppression of our emotions is what leads to disease, and our shame-based culture needs to get over that.

Suffice it to say, I *did* get into that cool, creative school, and Spirit wasn't short on humor or kismet. Turned out my space planning instructor had studied under H.H. Professor Lin Yun, in Berkeley, California, and she became the mentor I needed to start my professional journey into Feng Shui.

3

SHUI FUNDAMENTALS

"I didn't arrive at my understanding of the fundamental laws of the universe through my rational mind."

Albert Einstein

hen I first started learning Feng Shui with my new mentor, Marcy, she kept taking me back to the fundamentals. That was the part I kept intentionally skipping in all the books I was reading. I didn't care about yin and yang or this funny thing called Tao. I wanted to skip ahead to the good stuff, the energy stuff that taught me secret principles like fixing my front door. Because of my stubborn nature at the time, I failed to grasp the importance of these basics and how intrinsic they were to the constitution that makes Feng Shui what it is and allows it to work.

Yes, yes, yin and yang is balance, Chi is energy, and Tao is a funny word I can't pronounce. Let's get to the Bagua Map and start doing some hocus-pocus! I'm pretty certain the Five Element Theory continued to evade me until my current mentor, Katherine, but I learned them nonetheless. The fundamentals are the secret sauce that moves us towards energetic balance. If you don't grasp the fundamentals, your Feng Shui will stay in the shallows and never achieve the depths of where it can truly take you. When I first started learning Feng Shui, the fundamentals seemed irrelevant and archaic until I realized how vital they truly are. The central concept of achieving internal and external stability can only be accomplished through creating a balanced environment. In Feng Shui, it is the ultimate goal to balance both worlds, but that can only be done through a solid framework. It gives you the *how*. This is the mistake that many people make because they don't fully understand energy. We live in an instant-gratification world where a pill can fix everything and a cupcake can be dispensed in a vending machine at midnight. We rush to the finish line and miss the journey of exploration getting there.

When I truly grasped the beauty of the Tao Te Ching, my life changed forever. For me personally, learning the principles behind the Tao was the fastest way to cultivating my Chi. The Chinese always say, "Everything in accordance with the Tao." If you rush through everything and hurry to what you think is the good stuff, you miss the sweetness that is the best part of the fruit. Put another way, the Tao states, "A rolling stone gathers no moss."

Ironically, the one thing that evaded me, like the Five Element Theory, was the key to understanding why I was rushing through everything, which you'll learn about in this chapter. Luckily, much like the wisdom of Lao Tsu, my mentor, Marcy, was very patient—for the most part. She had seen the likes of me before and knew just how to handle me. She finally sat me down one day and told me I was not only being sloppy but breaking all the rules.

"You have to learn the rules like a master if you want to break them like a gregarious artist," she said, just like a true Master.

To my surprise, I excelled at design school. Here I thought I was entirely uncreative, and not only did I graduate with honors with a 4.0 average, but I also graduated a semester early. I was excited and ready to get to work! Despite feeling like a fish out of water during my interview process, I had quickly learned how to swim.

I started out by helping friends and neighbors with their design and Feng Shui, but my mama became my largest petri dish. Between my home and hers, it became my greatest lab of understanding energy medicine. Thank God for moms who are built to put up with their child's nonsense and do it with unconditional love and grace.

In 2001 tragedy struck. Every channel contained news of the Twin Towers. At the time, I was working at a furniture store, but on that day I didn't make it in. I couldn't take my attention away from the news. How could something like this happen in this day and age? How could there be so much hatred? In an effort to gain clarity and desperately find equanimity, I gained my greatest strength from Feng Shui and its medicine. Through ancient wisdom, I was able to tap into the Tao and escape the grips of fear. The beauty of Feng Shui is that it does not discriminate. Like sacred tonic, it illuminates and empowers you to eclipse despair and rise above. The best part is, you can start where you are, do it differently than everyone else, bring to it all your idiosyncrasies, and still succeed. And during such chaotic times, this mystical practice is more relevant today than ever.

You can approach Feng Shui at many different levels. You can go it alone, practice the techniques with friends, and share it with your family. You can scratch the surface by doing small experiments or take a deep dive and make it a daily enterprise. It will look different for everyone.

Go at it slowly, avoid skipping ahead, learn to speak her language, and remember, while we all occasionally need outside help and direction, your healing is an inside job, so tune in and listen. I've taught Feng Shui classes for years, worked with hundreds of clients and students, and I firmly believe that anyone can learn to influence the energy around them and learn Feng Shui. It's incredibly exciting to see the transformation my clients experience. But only through experimenting with it and honoring its core fundamentals will you develop a solid understanding of true Feng Shui and her medicine. Are you ready to learn the fundamentals? Let's do it!

WHAT IS CHI?

Chi is cosmic breath or life force. Without healthy Chi, you cannot be nourished or full. Furthermore, without Chi you'd cease to exist. It's literally the life force that makes you operate, just as electricity makes your toaster work. In our bodies, Chi is regarded as our personality or our true self. It's the life force that carries us, moving the body, operating the mind, and carrying our speech. If the flow is smooth and balanced, you will have good health and feel good. If the cosmic breath is blocked or stressed, your Chi will be disrupted and health will be affected, mood will alter, and you will likely not feel good.

While the relative state of your Chi continuously changes, the key throughout life is to keep it in balance so that it remains stable and healthy. Growth, movement and change, all part of the process of Tao, are necessary to produce dynamic vital Chi. Every day we witness change via the seasons, politics, beliefs, and even state of mind and emotions. Therefore, it's important to recognize that our environments are alive and interacting with us. Not only do our physical environments change as time passes, but so do we, which in turn influences the ebb and flow of Chi.

In the Black Sect tradition, we give a greater emphasis to subjective, intangible forces derived from intuition and inspiration. We call this transcendental. By cultivating your Chi through meditation and self care, you can reconcile energy in a powerful way and produce strong intuition. This is how you gain the artistry of auspicious placement of adjustments and an understanding of Chi within a space to improve your life and your environment. Your greatest weapon in achieving the highest Feng Shui result is you, and that can only be achieved with strong vibrant Chi. Through cultivation you get out of the logical mind and into the emotional intelligence of your body.

The view of Chi is wide ranging and all-encompassing. Not only is the flow of earth Chi taken into consideration and the Chi in our bodies, but it's also necessary to acknowledge how Chi is expressed in various situations. It's one of the many reasons the founder of BTB Feng Shui in the West, H.H. Professor Lin Yun, always expressed to "follow the Chi." When reviewing the Feng Shui, it can include the Chi of the land, the Chi within an establishment, the Chi of a person, and so on. For example, the Chi in Nashville is not the same as the Chi in New York, and vice versa. Chi is as individual as the location, institution, or the human that expresses it.

Respecting and understanding Chi is essential to understanding Feng Shui. Chi is easy to recognize since it is the vital force behind all things. An example of this would be driving through Beverly Hills. The Chi is literally abundant as opposed to driving through the back-roads anywhere in the U.S and seeing abandoned homes, deserted businesses, and other forgotten dwellings. Not only does the Chi *feel* different, it looks different.

According to traditional Chinese theory, there are five key factors that influence our lives and are seen as the chief life factors running our course. They are fate, luck, Feng Shui, karma, and education. Of course, the best circumstance would be to benefit from all five, however not all can be manipulated, and depending on the quality of each in your own life, some may be harder to achieve than others. The good news is, one life factor we have significant control over is our environment. The Chinese have long felt that Chi can influence one's destiny, and through Feng Shui we can change our Chi. By changing our Chi, we can improve our luck, gain knowledge, perform good deeds, and perhaps nudge fate towards a more favorable outcome. Hallelujah!

Fate is what we inherit when we come into this world. We are influenced by soul experience, and therefore it's thought of as immutable. But it can be massaged through free will. By using tools like astrology, intuition, meditation, and other esoteric tools like Feng Shui, you can better prepare for events and learn to how to be proactive instead of reactive. It may be time to grab your umbrella and rain coat, but the difference between an ordeal and an adventure is attitude!

Luck is like the Wheel of Fortune in the Tarot. It's the variations of ups and downs that we call life, and life is very cyclical. Some days are good, others not so much. However, if we address the ingredients that help shape luck, like practicing Feng Shui, doing good deeds, and cultivating Chi, we can drastically change how we perceive and experience life. By moderating those Below The Cross feelings and emotions, you can learn to maximize the ups and hopefully transcend the downs.

Feng Shui is all about increasing flow and abundance in all areas of your life through your personal Chi and environment. Through cultivation of your own Chi and that of your environment, you can influence the outcome of conditions in a favorable way, making them suitable to support you rather than hinder you.

Karma, in my opinion, is a word thrown around loosely in today's culture to encompass getting what you think is right or fair. But karma goes far beyond what outcome you think it should or shouldn't be. What you think doesn't really matter, because it's likely presenting itself through the lens of the ego. Simply put, karma is balancing the scales via cause and effect from your actions, AKA, your energy. In Feng Shui, you can wield better karma by doing good deeds and staying in those Above the Cross Emotions. A bad mood or perpetual fits of rage create a string of bad luck, and you'll start to accumulate bad karma. It's the old adage of getting up on the wrong side of the bed. If one thing goes wrong, you have a choice to allow it to snowball out of control into one negative event after another or change its course. Yet another reason to cultivate your Chi and actively participate in staying Above the Cross.

Education can play a key role in not only changing fate but also creates circumstances for better luck, improving your environment, balancing karma, and smoothing your Chi. Through education, we create new opportunities for ourselves and others. As Maya Angelou so famously stated, "When you know better, you do better." And when you know better, you move from knowledge, which is often passed down through other peoples perceived views, to wisdom, which comes from your inner truth that's learned over time through better education.

Maintaining, moderating, and enhancing Chi flow is the underlying intention in Feng Shui. Good Chi flow in an environment improves the Chi of its residents and vice versa. Understanding Chi is essential to understanding the health of any home, office, establishment, or piece of land. In many ways, even though I never got my medical degree, I act as a space doctor fixing environmental ills. It is up to me, through my own cultivation, to discern the pulse of Chi within a space. And only through experience and the artistry that is Feng Shui have I learned how to smooth, balance, and harmonize Chi and speak her language. Through your own cultivation, you'll be able to do the same!

TAO AND YIN AND YANG

Tao is an instinctive process that links humans to the heartbeat of the Universe. In other words, it is a reflection of the natural way we humans tap into the eternal rhythm or music of the cosmos. The concept of Tao emerged from the ancient Chinese observations of nature, her rhythms, and our relationship to it. While studying Tao, they determined two things: nature is constantly in flux, and the fate of their crops depended on *the way* of nature's expressions. Furthermore, humans and nature follow the same law or path. This truth, or law, establishes that Tao creates complete wholeness only when it stems from its opposite, which can only be achieved through interacting tug and pull, like up and down, light and dark, or hot and cold.

Much like the Wheel of Fortune of luck, it reminds you that the wheel is always turning and life is in a state of constant change. Tao is constant, cyclical change. Like the seasons, summer always precedes fall, which in turn leads to winter. By understanding the Tao, you can use Feng Shui to strike balance and equilibrium in your environment.

From the Tao came two primordial, complimentary forces known as yin and yang. These two opposing positive and negative forces act together in constant motion, creating a tug of war of balanced energy. They represent the precept of opposites, or the duality of extreme that makes room for distinctions like black and white, up and down, or front to back.

Yin's, the feminine, passive principle relates to qualities like dark and cool. It is the Earth and the moon. While Yang, the male active principle, relates to light and hot. It is the sun and the sky. Together they combine in nature to produce all existing harmonious relationships, otherwise known as Tao. They are the epitome of opposites, and Feng Shui concentrates on nourishing Chi by executing a balance between these two extremes to achieve harmony.

When we experience dramatic architecture that goes to the extreme, we can feel the disproportionate yang energy, because it feels aggressive and active. Or, a room that is incredibly dark with low ceilings and filled with clutter can be felt as far too yin, because it feels dark, stagnant and passive. It's important to observe, however, that the polarities of yin and yang are not absolute. The artistry in a practiced eye can find the yin in the yang and the yang in the yin. As you further your understanding of energy, you'll learn how to perceive nuance. Through refinement and other distinctions, you'll learn how to read the Chi of people and environments, furthering comfort and suitability over time by way of Feng Shui.

Yin	Yang
Feminine	Masculine
Cool	Hot
Dark	Light
Back	Front
Earth	Sky
Moon	Sun

Yin and yang is what links us to our environments by dividing everything into complementary dualities. Grasping the connection, coupled with Tao, you can maintain inner and external balance and improve your fortune and luck. It's important to say that the influence of Tao touches everything in nearly all aspects of design. Feng

Shui inspires us to seek its wisdom to bring us harmony and balance, even when we are lost in seasons of life that might appear as chaos.

THE FIVE ELEMENTS

In addition to being influenced by Chi and yin and yang, we are also influenced through the manifestation of the five elements. The five elements function as powerful change agents that stimulate and shape our daily lives. These are not just physical substances but energetic forces that permeate our universe. The beauty in understanding the elements can be lost in their simple physical expressions. Meaning, the five elements go far beyond wood, metal, water, earth, and fire. They are not only the building blocks of everything physical in our world, but they manifest in countless ways and combinations around us. Understanding their natural order can help you develop a deep understanding of how Chi expresses itself. This is not only something you see, but also something you *feel*.

Each element has its own quality and essence. This essence can be applied to houses, plots of land, decor, and even people, characterizing all matter. The ability to assess, define, and balance an element reveals exactly what needs to be done in order to bring an environment or person back into balance. When elements are out of balance, it can be easy to feel off in an environment, but you may not be able to put your finger on why. When elements are out of balance in personal Chi, we can see lack of discernment, indecisiveness, and self righteousness to name a few.

Each of the five elements is full of associations like colors, shapes, times, qualities, and personality. For example, when it comes to colors, metal is grey, water is black, wood is green or blue, fire is red, and earth is yellow. This forms the language for interpreting and directing their expression in a positive fashion. Together, these elements mutually create or destroy one another when placed in a particular order through cycles. In Feng Shui, these two forces create a subsequent relationship between the elements as a powerful way to stir Chi. These cycles are known as the Creative Cycle and the Destructive Cycle.

In the creative cycle, metal produces water, water feeds wood, wood fuels fire, fire produces earth, and earth creates metal. In the destructive cycle, wood uproots earth, earth dams water, water destroys fire, fire melts metal, and metal chops wood. Metal is often seen as round, water seen as wavy, wood is expansive and columnar, fire is pointy or triangular, and earth rectangular or square.

For the purposes of keeping the elements understandable and simple, the most important thing to remember is that one cycle generates and the other eliminates, but both sequences are positive forces in Feng Shui. Many students see the word destructive and think it destroys Chi or is negative. The sequence simply describes natural events, like Tao, and how we can use that power to manipulate Chi. How cool is that?

When learning the elements, consider their relationship to one another and contemplate how the energy behind these forces can be positively used. For example, utilizing color in an auspicious cycle can enhance Chi. The color green represents growth of a new shoot and vitality; therefore, if a client lacks vitality in their life, I can intentionally use the color green to energetically align their home for better well-being. But consider further using a creative cycle like metal, (white) water (black) and wood (green) to powerfully charge a space with energy and manipulate Chi. This is how you achieve design that's energy aligned, and it's a space that feels as good as it looks!

Learn to distinguish the elements by their properties in terms of shape, color, and material. Experiment by locating these elements in your own home or in photos. When creating a cycle, you can start anywhere, and you only need three of the elements to powerfully shift the Chi. You can use them if a space needs growth, feels off, or perhaps has been abandoned or carries negative energy. Utilizing a cycle gets things moving quickly and is considered an immediate and potent infusion of Chi, or energy medicine.

In Feng Shui, people also express five element Chi. Some traditions hold that a person only has one elemental ruling, but in Black

Sect theory, we each have all five in our constitution. Most of us harbor within that constitution a dominant element that expresses our personality and behaviors. Like all things, it is a delicate dance to not dip into the shadow sides of unbalanced Chi. Ahem, like a student who stubbornly chooses not to learn the fundamentals of Feng Shui and *rushing* to the hocus-pocus, which is a classic wood personality out of balance. This is why it is imperative that you take the time to cultivate your Chi daily and stay in those Above the Cross emotions. You need to balance, recalibrate, and adjust your Chi daily. This isn't to just smooth things out, but to also keep your Chi dynamic, expressive, and healthy to respect your unique individuality.

Here are some typical traits of elemental Chi.

Metal - When in balance, finds organizing quite easy, is articulate, refined, and structured. Typically has a strong sense of self. Loves beauty and simplicity. When out of balance, they have a strong sense to be right, can become controlling and obsessive, and fears chaos.

Water - When in balance, can be self contained, likes deep thinking, visionary, and loves to seek truth. They love solitude and privacy. When out of balance, there is a fear of being vulnerable, of being exposed, and a fear of sharing. They don't want their ideas to be stolen because their ideas are very important to them. They can get lost and drown in the data, books, and philosophies.

Wood - When in balance, they are self-confident, ambitious, and ingenious. They are actionary and love to innovate. When out of balance, they become highly impatient, move at a high rate of speed, rush, become intolerant and stubborn.

Fire - When in balance, they are illuminated, bright, and affectionate. They have a warmth to them and fierce intuition. They are optimistic and playful. Their charisma can be quite seductive. When out of balance, they can quickly lose their sense of self. They lack discernment, become overwhelmed, anxious, and confused.

Earth - When in balance, they are extremely stable, caring, and predictable. They love community and to be needed. They are generous and very caring. When out of balance, they tend to hoard and fear not having enough. They hate change, can easily get lost in the details of others, and can get obsessed with pleasing others.

At first, seeing the expression of the elements will seem foreign to you. Practice noticing the elemental combinations in the things that surround you. Whether in an environment, a building, or a person, everything holds this Chi, and you will soon become fluent in describing the elements everywhere you go.

THE QUINTESSENTIAL FENG SHUI TOOL: THE BAGUA MAP

Now that we have the basics of Chi, yin yang cosmology, and the Tao in order, we've graduated to learning about the Bagua Map. This map delineates what areas of your home have to do with your life. Remember earlier when I explained that your home is a third skin? That concept comes from this theology, where energy within your home combines in a special pattern and becomes a spiritual expression of energy in your life. This map or grid of nine areas can be drafted on a plot of land, over a home, in a car, on a person, or within a room and reveals clues as to what may be showing up in your life.

In the simplest of terms, this map is an interpretation of how the universe manifests in your life through your home. This is where the rubber meets the road when practicing what I initially called hocus-pocus and why I was so eager to skip all the other stuff to get here. Learning the Bagua Map serves to solve a lot of problems. It's uncanny how often you'll see the way you are living, or the way your home is designed, correlates to something within the Bagua Map. Ultimately, the Bagua Map helps you discover all the parts of your home that correlate with your life and shows you it's all of equal importance.

The Bagua Map can be applied to just about any fixed shape. The goal is to apply it to said shape and review the individual gua locations. The individual boxes are called a gua (g-wa), and they are the basis for determining what areas are weak or strong in your life. Each gua corresponds to a different life area, such as family, career, or health. In symbolic language, the guas represent the forces that create, control, or destroy, possibility and opportunity in your life.

The Bagua Map

Main Entrance

The word Bagua literally means eight sides. Traditionally, the Bagua Map is an eight-sided octagon with what are known as eight trigrams or life areas. A trigram is a basic building block from the ancient text, *The I Ching, or Book of Changes*. The Bagua Map is an arrangement of eight trigrams (guas) in your life that represent helpful people, career, knowledge, children, partnership, fame, wealth, family, and knowledge, and they encompass a center, or tai chi. Stemming from the founder of the Chou dynasty, King Wen, we are seen in the tai chi center, receiving the flow of Chi, or blessings. This allows you to receive your karma, transcend pain and suffering, and come to a place of allowing. Experiencing the flow of Chi in this way, we learn how to understand ourselves as a grounded whole. Only when we are here can we transform ourselves through Feng Shui.

The Bagua Map serves as a tool to couple various components in your home with connection to areas in your physical world with astute accuracy. Overlaying the map onto your environment addresses why issues may be showing up, how to take action, and where to do it. Each gua represents an enormous constellation of meaning starting with attributes like color, seasons, elements, patterns, organs, and other traits. It is important to remember that each gua holds a plethora of meaning and mysticism, and they go far beyond the single concept or keyword given to them. For instance, the partnership gua goes far beyond its single-word meaning. The partnership gua represents the earth, which has the ability to absorb all things. It's indicative of the matriarch, has an ability to receive, and speaks for the internal organs. Viewing it simply as the place to boost your marriage possibilities would be futile because it is that, and so much more.

The Bagua Map is a way to improve Chi in your environment by applying philosophical and transcendental principles that are rooted in ancient mysticism. The purpose of the map is to guide you towards a better life by interpreting where energy or Chi is stuck, stagnant, dormant, or even harmful. Superimposing this tool onto a room, entire building, or plot of land exposes the issue and acts as a conduit to change it. Understanding the Bagua and its mysticism allows you to create a relationship to your home beyond the norm and enables you to manipulate your luck and destiny.

The application of this tool is quite simple. Draw a sketch of your home and superimpose two vertical lines and two horizontal lines to create nine boxes. One of the most important rules to applying the Bagua Map is placing it according to the front door location. The front door, translated as "the mouth of Chi" is pivotal in getting your calculation correct. No matter how infrequently the front door is used, it determines where all nine boxes go, not the side door, back door, or garage door.

When the Bagua is placed on a room, building, or plot of land, the entrance will always land in one of three possible locations: knowledge, career, or helpful people. By applying the Bagua Map according to its entrance, it's possible that it will expose ill-shapes. An ill-shape is anything that creates what's called a missing area or missing gua. We will get into this further in Chapter 5, but a missing piece creates an odd shape which can create a multitude of problems.

By and large, the Bagua Map is one of the most results-oriented tools in Feng Shui. By correlating your home, office, or land with the energy medicine of transcendental mysticism, you summon the blessings and vitality this map can bring you. The Bagua Map shows you how to overcome obstacles, take action, and invite positive change and good fortune into your life. To work with the Bagua Map, or any of the fundamentals for that matter, with an open heart is to stand in the presence of the Universe and all her wisdom and say, "I am ready, open, and willing for all that you have to offer me." Unfortunately, our own blindness can get in the way on our path of enlightenment. There are many highways to find enlightenment, and Feng Shui is only one of them. Each pilgrim must find their own way out of ignorance.

LET'S GET OUR FACTS STRAIGHT, AVIDYA!

As mentioned in earlier chapters, some struggle with the theory of Feng Shui, passing it off as sheer superstition. Others simply dabble in it. In my opinion, Western culture has treated Feng Shui a bit like an entertaining party trick—a metaphysical cornucopia of sorts to play in a spiritual sandbox without fully understanding its depth and wisdom. I should know. I attacked it in this way too, skipping ahead to get to what I thought was the good stuff. Let me tell you from first-hand experience, you will find that skipping ahead or rushing this is ineffective and trivial. To get to the marrow, you have to live it, breathe, it and experience it fully. This is Feng Shui for the Soul™. Unfortunately, I have found that most will only scratch the surface experimenting with it as something to do once or twice to say they've tried it, then move on to the next shiny thing. But to truly embrace

Heaven and Earth and touch Samadhi, or union with the divine, Feng Shui isn't something you try; it's a lifestyle you become.

In our frantic, frenetic world many of us get caught up in the shallows, or what the mystics call the Maya. Stemming from a Sanskrit word, Maya is defined as the cosmic illusion, where the power in creation intentionally exposes us to limitation and division so that we are forced to look beyond the veil by way of spiritual matter to discover oneness which is true reality. The constant battle is that it is up to us to decipher and read between the lines to perceive what is real. To me, Feng Shui gives us the spiritual tools to see and understand the silence between the notes. Perfect union of the individualized soul with infinite spirit is what gives us an overall oneness and meaning in life, not the material things or energetic clutter you fill your life with. Feng Shui is the spiritual matter that fills the void; therefore, Samadhi is what we should all aspire to accomplish. Only in this way can you extend yourself beyond the illusion of what is, and experience all that is. Over the last twenty years, Feng Shui has been my Samadhi. But if you are caught up in the illusion of it all how in the world do you do it?

In both Buddhism and Hinduism, the thing that traps us in said limitations and divisions, preventing Samadhi, is Avidya, the delusion or ignorance from all that is. Avidya is sometimes translated as "incorrect understanding." Buddhists say Avidya is a misunderstanding of the nature of reality. However, this does not suggest failure or wrongdoing. It simply suggests that your Avidya is a spiritual ignorance, or blindspot, that is preventing you from connecting to the divine and true Self.

The realization of Avidya comes from the Yoga Sutras, widely regarded as the authoritative text on yoga. These sutras or "threads" of wisdom offer guidelines for living a meaningful and purposeful life. Patanjali, the Indian sage who is believed to have authored the Yoga Sutras, describes Avidya as the first of the five obstacles, or kleshas, that block the spiritual path. By destroying Avidya, the other kleshas become less an issue, and it is my belief that, through Feng Shui, you can begin to see past the illusions. However, if unwilling to see spiritual matter in this way, it can take you an entire lifetime to overcome it. Avidya is the master who obscures the true Self, firmly establishing that meaning can only be found in ego, and non-spiritual matter via Maya. If you buy into this theory, which is the lock preventing change, you will find it hard to overcome your Avidya, or your blindspot. In order to reach the soul, you're gonna have to rise above the Maya and acknowledge your blindspots so you can embrace your own Samadhi, because that's where the good stuff lies, not the superficial hocus-pocus! Embracing Feng Shui as spiritual matter is the only way to enhance your quality of life, improve your environment, and transcend all suffering. That is Feng Shui for the Soul™.

4

TOP 5 DISRUPTORS™

"The pleasure of the soul appears to be found in the journey of discovery, the unfolding revelation of expanded insight and experience."
Anthony Lawler

After three years of living in BoBo, our now well-loved home in Northern California, it was time for us to say good-bye, and we moved to Las Vegas for a quick minute. It seemed like a perfect time too, as California was struggling with an energy crisis, rolling black outs were sweeping the state causing state wide mania, and the Governor had tripled taxes, which furthered frustration and anger. While I was sad to leave BoBo, I knew my next chapter awaited me.

I met mom at the Las Vegas airport and, before meeting the real estate agent to see all the possible new houses, we stopped off for a quick breakfast at Denny's.

"So do you have an idea of what you want?" Mom said.

"Nope, but I sure as heck know what I don't want!" I quickly replied.

At this stage in the game, I was well versed in the "F" word. For three glorious years, I was glued to Marcy, my mentor, like white on rice, learning about Feng Shui. While lovin' on BoBo, I fell in love with the idea of a healthy home that heals. I would soon come to realize, however, not everyone wanted to be apart of this, nor cared about the "F" word as much as I did.

As Miss Dyson, the real estate agent, chauffeured mom and me around Las Vegas showing us homes she considered to be "very suitable," I soon became the client she feared and loathed. She would pull up to a house, and I would refuse to even get out of the car. Homes that had a bathroom right off the entrance would cause me to walk right back out of the house without so much as entering fully into the home, and anything with the words "divorced, foreclosed, or health issues" were absolute No's. One house we walked in had all the cabinets ripped out, and the upstairs bathroom had a perfect iron mark on the cultured marble as if, out of spite, the previous homeowner said, "You may be kicking me out, but I will imprint my anger right here to show you my distaste." I could feel the anger and sadness. Umm, that's a hard no!

Even though I worked through many negative issues with BoBo, I didn't want to buy another house that had major negative imprints. I wanted something a little easier this time around. But when it comes to energy, you can't always control what's vibrationally aligned to you, or what vibrationally needs you. I ended up attracting the very house that needed the most love in the neighborhood, if not the entire city.

She had great bones, and was much younger than BoBo, but she was filled with anger and anxiety. After a month of us moving in, my then husband and I quickly fell into erratic energy soup. I tried everything to make my home healthy, but our bed was out of command, meaning we couldn't see the door, and we were constantly slammed with anxiety, mood swings, and things coming out of nowhere, a classic sign of being out of command. We also had two massive knife-edges, or wall corners, framing our bed, further contributing to our anxiety, insomnia, and arguing. Within three months of living here, our health took a toll, money became erratic, and our moods were out of control. We both lost our jobs, and for the first time in my life, I experienced pure dread and fear around money and life. One of our vehicles got repossessed and arguing was constant. I even fell down the stairs and twisted my ankle, twice. These are classic signs that the energy is not right, especially if these behaviors are unusual. I would later learn that, when a space has strong energy imprints and residual energy left over from its previous occupants, it creates what's known as predecessor Chi.

Even though this home was built in the nineties, it had seen far worse energy than BoBo had. Unbeknownst to us at the time of purchase, my research revealed there had been six previous owners, and this poor gal had seen divorce, suicide, overdose, massive addictions, gambling, and mental illness. Holy bananas! While I seemed like a sure bet to help her rise back to her glory, my Chi was not strong enough to heal this trifecta of chaos soup. Ultimately, life got in the way, I got worn down, and we decided to toss in the towel and move.

Even though we only lived with Goldie for less than a year, she greatly influenced me. It wasn't until a few years later, while working with a medical intuitive, that I learned how to become more in tuned to my environment through my heart energy. Understanding how to discern this language made me better equipped to decipher Feng Shui wisdom, and I realized my home and I were not meshing well, and she was acting out. Her energy was enraged, and my husband and I were not powerful enough to heal her. I just didn't know enough at the time. I knew the principles of Feng Shui, but my Chi was not powerful enough to overcome the dark, heavy energy that inhabited this space. This would become a pivotal learning experience for me in cultivating my own Chi. I look back now and sigh. If only I knew then what I know now. Today I could go into that space like Wonder Woman, kick ass and take names. *Ka-pow!* I'd whip that house's energy into shape in a New York minute! But as Theodore Roosevelt stated, "Do what you can, with what you have, from where you are." Each beautiful home teaches me something new, and for that I am forever grateful.

HEADED TO GOD'S COUNTRY

My spouse was not a big believer in Feng Shui. In fact, he thought it was downright hooey. But I knew that Vegas was a stepping stone for us. It felt like a holding pattern until the right thing opened up. But until it opened up, we needed a place to live to figure things out. Goldie had been a traumatizing experience for both of us. It's hard to explain, but we left feeling exhausted, stressed, and frazzled. It was hard to shake off. Our temporary space was better, but I was beginning to realize a lot of the energy I was picking up was not only from previous occupants but the energy of Vegas itself. We ended up living in our rental home for about eight months. While there, I set a clear intention that our next move would not be in the state of Nevada. I went to a local bookstore and bought a huge map of the United States and placed it in our laundry room. I wanted it there because every day we would be forced to see it as we walked to the garage. Then I placed a mirror over the fireplace to create yin yang energy in the center of the house. Every day I would focus on these intentions and tell the universe we were ready for our next move. However, I was about to learn yet another key Feng Shui lesson. My energy was always off in Vegas. I was in a constant state of anxiety and stress. And because I still had not mastered how to cultivate my own personal Chi, I was personally emanating incoherence into my Feng Shui intentions. It's like tuning into a radio station that has a lot of static. No matter how hard you try to listen, ultimately you're going to miss things. This will make it harder to manifest. But I was determined. Even if my radio signal was filled with static, I decided forward is forward. Every day I kept telling my husband that we'd be getting a call or a message about our next move. Then one day as I was walking through the laundry room, I stopped and looked at the map. Without hesitation I said under my breath, today is the day. I called my husband and said, "I have a feeling we're going to get a call today and a new job offer." Sure enough, that afternoon my husband received an offer from his company to take over a position in Sugarland, Texas.

The funny thing about vibration is that, not only do you manifest your reality, but you're the captain of your fate, even if you're not entirely sure how to steer your ship. Your destiny knows the way, and it will guide you like a faithful leader if you listen. If your Chi is strong, you will correctly intuit the guidance and ride along with destiny as doors open, meeting side by side with fate. It may disguise itself as disappointment or scary change, but trust that your bus ticket is taking you in the right direction. To me, Vegas seemed disappointing and scary, but ultimately it's the stepping stone that eventually got us to Nashville.

While mentally I was ready to move to Texas, spiritually it didn't feel right. I could feel that it wasn't the place for us. When I looked at the Shui of our rental home, there were a few things I now call disruptors that were affecting clarity and direction. Despite my husband not being on board with my esoteric ways, even after witnessing it first hand, he was on board with figuring out where we were going. So I decided to do more Feng Shui. I adjusted a bathroom, our bedroom, and cleaned our front door. Within twelve hours of me making the adjustments, we received the call, "You're going to Nashville!" Within two weeks of receiving that call we were officially headed to God's Country.

Within six months of moving to Nashville, we met our new home, Loho. In the Indo-European language of Maharashtra, India, Loho means to have a great fondness for something. Our new home had depth and strength, and she felt like none of the other homes we'd inhabited. She introduced herself to me immediately, and I did have a great fondness for her and all we would accomplish.

Right after moving into Loho, a college girlfriend named Sarah contacted me to let me know she'd gotten married and they were about to embark on buying a house. Due to several failed relationships and other obstacles in her life, she wanted to ensure she got the energy right. Admittedly, I was surprised to get her call. She had never seemed interested in energy medicine prior to this time. My concern was that she was getting caught up in the party trick of Feng Shui, rushing to what she thought might be the superficial answer to her happily ever after. However, it also shows the allure of what energy can do. In its own mysterious way, it steeps into your bones and whispers into your heart without you realizing it. It's not something you witness, but it is something that's felt, and unbeknownst to Sarah, she felt something and it was starting to stir within her.

I THINK SHE'S LOST HER MARBLES

Years prior, while still living in BoBo, Sarah had thrown a party for me to celebrate my wedding engagement. During the renovation period, alongside the panic attacks, I had also suffered random fever blisters. I had never had a fever blister, but during this renovation I had several. They were painful, and they were always in the middle of my lower lip. No surprise, I would discover that this was yet another form of communication from BoBo. Remember my "mouth of Chi" had been obstructed and boarded up, and my front door was smack dab in the middle of the front of my house. As soon as work began to create an operational door, my mouth healed and I've never had a fever blister since. Ever.

It was during this party, however, that I was healing from my last fever blister. I shared my Feng Shui story with Sarah, about the power of energy and this thing called the "mouth of Chi." I also shared how this energy can manifest in our physical lives, like me having a fever blister. "The cool thing," I shrieked, "is if you work with it, it will change your life."

My excitement was palpable; Sarah's was a mix of "I guess there could be a correlation," and "She's lost her marbles." I'm pretty sure Sarah was in the camp of "She's lost her marbles." But without her realizing it, the seed had been planted at that party. It whispered into her heart and touched her soul and laid dormant until now. That seed may start with suspicion, gestate as moderate hope and, if you're lucky, turns to absolute truth. But the thing to remember is, all seeming obstacles to a successful mystical practice start with you. When you are ready, suspicion awakens to absolute truth.

GAINING SPIRITUAL WISDOM TAKES TIME

In order for Feng Shui to work, you gotta be willing to do the work—the real work. In practical terms, most people view Feng Shui as a tool on how to place a physical object or how to manage and organize their clutter. While this is a form of energy medicine, as mentioned in earlier chapters, Feng Shui goes much deeper. Going deeper requires you to embrace your own mystical side, put logic aside, and create your own inner Woodstock.

When I asked Sarah what she was hoping to gain through her Feng Shui consultation, she surprised me by saying that she wanted to have a soul connection with her new home. *Bingo!* I thought. *She's willing to do the work.* Since getting married she had embarked on a spiritual path seeking to lift the lens and find truth. According to Dr. Hawkins in *Power VS Force,* this is the point that the soul reaches courage and starts to lift the veil of maya.

When I explained to her that this would require ceremony and other rituals, she was in, and I was excited. But before we could get to the offerings, I would have to draft a checklist of everything she needed to look for in her new home.

I put together a worksheet of everything one should look for when buying a new house. Following a month of time, hours of research, and careful consideration, I developed a list of over two hundred items to look for in her new home. I was proud of my cataloged list. That is, until I sent it to Sarah and in her blunt nature she replied, "What the hell am I supposed to do with this?" In Sarah's opinion, the list was far too complex, too long, and would take a year for a newbie like her to locate a "Where's Waldo" approach to Feng Shui. To this day, we still have an inside joke. If she doesn't understand me when I am geeking out about Feng Shui, she'll say, "Hold up, where's Waldo?"

Ultimately, it would take me another six years to figure out the answer. No one ever said becoming enlightened would be easy or quick. It was a grueling task trying to narrow down what I thought was the most important things to consider within a home. But after careful review of past clients, their testimonials, results of my own, and the sheer magic that is Feng Shui, I developed my proprietary system called The Top Five Disruptors™. And I have my house Loho to thank for this enlightenment. It was my direct relationship with her that allowed me the cultivation to birth this new system. Each house teaches me something new and allows my soul to expand, and your home will too!

The Top Five Disruptors™ are the rudimentary elements to look for to hone in on what can be fixed right away to invoke change. Plus, it's a terrific starting point so you take action with confidence. But keep in mind, it's the combination of ceremony and belief in mysticism that's the secret sauce, which we'll learn more about in the next chapter. Without this ingredient, you can't touch the primordial light and connect Heaven and Earth. You can't experience the magic that is Feng Shui.

AN INTRODUCTION TO THE TOP FIVE DISRUPTORS™

When you start working with this magical art, you'll quickly realize that it's an intrinsically woven system rich in metaphor, symbolism, and even omens. Move your bed and you'll instantly reduce risk of insomnia and anxiety; hang a mirror and you'll eliminate drained Chi in a bathroom; hang a wind chime and you can change the shape of your home. Certain things represent symbology that can have major influence on the outcome of your luck and fate, but it takes an open and curious mind.

In order to have strong health, good finances, or a loving relationship, certain factors have to follow a specific energy alignment with nature. Our ultimate goal in all that we do is to keep our environments open, welcoming, and smooth to allow Chi to flow easily.

In ancient China, the Chinese believed that if they wanted to have a *sweet* life they needed to make sugary offerings to Buddha. In addition, they understood the importance of honoring the earth by being stewards of God's soil, and that proper care and maintenance of their land was crucial to survival. While these principles may seem archaic and simple compared to today's modern world, they are nonetheless profound. Feng Shui has been passed down with honor and it's a tool that's evolved into the principles found in this book so that you can have a sweet life too. I often say that without my ancestors, I could not call myself a Feng Shui practitioner, nor could I have authored this book!

There are many principles that make up the backbone of good Feng Shui. For the sake of making Feng Shui easy, approachable, and actually doable, I developed this system of The Top Five Disruptors™ to get you started. This system is by no means complete, but it sets the tone and a strong foundation upon which your Feng Shui journey can begin. And my hope is that you try it, fall in love with her magic, and continue to learn more. The top 5 are:

1. **Front Door:** The front door is where all Chi enters your home, meanders, and feeds every gua in your life. In Feng Shui, it's known as the "mouth of Chi." If this area isn't used, is blocked, dirty, or marginally operating, you're going to experience feeling stuck in your life, and your health will suffer. Twenty years ago, my front door is the reason I got into Feng Shui. At the time, mine was located in the career gua and had been boarded up for close to a year due to construction. I kept having breathing fits, which I later discovered were panic attacks, and I had a fever blister, which I'd never had in my life. My "mouth" was being affected by the "mouth" of my home.

2. **Shape:** Shape is incredibly important to any building. Ideally, the shape should be square or rectangular. It's said that round is ideal too, but who the heck has a round house? Not many! If the shape is odd, like an "L", "U," or irregular in some way, it will hinder the way Chi can flow throughout a space.

3. **Knife-edge:** A knife-edge is any sharp protrusion coming at you from a wall corner, piece of furniture, sculpture, a neighbor's house or it could be an entire building corner. A knife-edge has been scientifi-cally proven to have a different frequency to it, creating sharp shooting Chi. This is important to pay attention to at your bed, desk, or stove, and any area you spend a large amount of time at should never have a knife-edge. If a building has a large knife-edge coming at

your business or home, it can project that sharp shooting frequency at your building and wreck havoc on your life.

4. **Bathrooms:** The average bathroom has three to five drains. The purpose of a bathroom is literally elimination, so guess where your Chi goes? Discovering where your bathrooms land according to the Bagua Map can be an eye-opening experience. Do you find yourself saying, "My family drains me so much?" Well, I bet you have a bathroom sitting on your family gua. Pay attention to the things you say, as they are great clues when unearthing the mystical properties of Feng Shui.

5. **Command:** When I first learned Feng Shui, this was the easiest concept for me to grasp. Mainly because I had been in med school and understood the concept behind fight or flight and the parasympathetic nervous system. Being in command means you can always see the door. It's simple evolution built into your DNA. Back in the caveman days, we would hunker down in a cave and place our backs to the cave for safety reasons. It allowed us to be prepared if a tiger wanted to eat us. Command is also important at your bed, desk, and stove. Being out of command can really affect your health, make you anxious, and can destroy your work flow.

CONSCIOUS LIVING

To do this work requires that you empty your mind of all thoughts that separate you from the universe, which means most of them. In order to capture the essence and transformative relevance of The Top Five Disruptors™, it requires you to live your life consciously and fully. Learn to be present in your soul work without your ego. It can be easy to shrug off the list as too simple or doubt its spiritual significance. As humans, we love to overcomplicate things and question its applicability. But a Spiritual practice and steadfast belief is necessary to turn ordinary matter into that of great illumination and ever-renewing fulfillment.

Two years ago, I worked with a gentleman looking to buy a house to expand his business. This home would be used for retreats, holidays, and a place for business executives. He supplied me with a floor plan of a home he loved but it was chock-full with energy kinks. The front door, shape, and commanding positions were all compromised. I recommended that he either keep looking or implement Feng Shui energy medicine to remedy the issues. He disregarded my advice. The house he chose was large and impressive but riddled with energy flaws. I explained that he would encounter partnership issues, anxiety, and financial distress, and retreats would likely have unforeseen events happen to them, assuming that they took place at all! Ultimately, his plans would feel like an uphill battle. Within six months of purchasing his home, he struggled with retreats not filling up, retreats being cancelled, resources being taxed and anxiety. Then the entire house flooded due to a pipe bursting.

SPIRITUAL TRADITION

It always fascinates me when people hire me and then decide not to take the advice. When I looked back at my notes to review the retreat house while writing this book, many of the things that ended up happening were things that could have been avoided. The pipe breaking was definitely an unforeseen event, and that one event alone created enormous financial distress and anxiety. So why do people choose to ignore wisdom? In our modern times, we have lost touch to the natural rhythms of life. Logic precedes our very existence and technology consumes our time. We once lived in the depths of ancestral tradition and carried forth the thread of a collective soul through ceremony. It was through connection, family, ceremony, and ritual that we touched our souls and found spiritual meaning in our lives. The mystical made sense to us. Today, however, we live in what I call the shallows. When Sarah spoke of wanting Feng Shui to help avoid failed relationships and other obstacles in her life, she spoke as if the world had fallen against her, a side effect of living in the shallows and lacking meaning in life. When the business man was given a list of ceremonies and remedies to help the energy in his new home, he chose to argue that, logically, what I was saying was impossible. And the events that ultimately happened, according to him, well, that was pure coincidence. But was it? Rather than seeing life through a Below the Cross lens, what if instead we all chose to view it as the necessary path to arrive to where we are today? For Sarah, getting married and about to buy a beautiful new home. For the business man, perhaps wisdom when he buys a home in the future. Without a spiritual practice, it can be hard to see the correlation and the opportunity for growth.

Finding meaning in your life will only occur when you tap into the spiritual matter that fills the voids through a spiritual practice. For some, that can be found in the bonds of family; for others, it's religion, or spirituality, or getting out in nature, or a combination of it all. One of my favorite things about Chinese New Near is it's immersed in rich family customs that span thousands of years. It's a festival that celebrates the Lunar New Year, but at its core, it's all about family reunion and coming together to celebrate ancestral Chi. The festival includes moon gazing, lighting lanterns, lion dances, and celebrating peace. Imagine gathering with grandmothers, mothers, and daughters to share this generational experience! It's the epitome of the triple goddess trinity of crone, mother, and maiden celebrated annually.

The lantern festival originated when emperor Ming, a devout Buddhist, discovered that monks would light candles to honor Buddha. So the Emperor ordered that everyone light candles and hang lanterns to show tribute to Buddha. Many cultures have assorted practices similar to this that observe the seasons, value family, and honor tradition. And these traditions are passed down. While the Western world has its traditions, they are still quite young and superficial. In fact, many of our traditions revolve around drinking and consumerism, as if the celebration has been given a hall pass for bad behavior. And let me be clear, there is nothing wrong with the celebrations we have. However, many people have no idea what the celebration is really about. Tradition and ceremony are often key ingredients to achieving spiritual samadhi, or a state of absolute joy. But it can't be treated as a party trick or something you dabble in. In order to do this, you have to learn to flow with the cosmic current, find your Tao, and in doing this, you lose your labels and limitations to see the bigger picture. Otherwise, you stay caught up in the shallows thinking life is constantly attacking you. Moreover, in the modern world we have been conditioned to shy away from tradition and ceremony because we've been taught that it's antiquated and weird.

Bottom line, Feng Shui is a spiritual practice. It is a tradition that is thousands of years old. It is not a religion but a way of life. It is a tool that brings you closer to a higher state of being. In a culture that dotes on collecting knowledge via fast news and social media, and then creating an opinion from it, turn instead to ancient wisdom and tradition to seek your true light and gain real wisdom. If you are going to change your way of thinking about reality and move past your own Avidya, you have to facilitate your own journey into initiation through experience and stop trying to think your way through everything.

TO TOUCH THE PRIMORDIAL LIGHT OR TI

In Andean Shaman civilization Ti speaks for light. Ti creates beauty, brings fortune, and heals the sick. Ti is the source of power for Shamans, but it can just as easily destroy if not properly used and honored. *Wow.* Sounds a lot like Chi, doesn't it? The power all of us holds, whether you call it Ti, Prana, Chi, or divine cosmic breath, is being lost because more and more people are becoming distracted by trivial shallows and not honoring ancient wisdom. Sarah was not experiencing bad luck for the sake of bad luck. She was perceiving that her life was not full based on artificial notions that don't exist. And neither was the business man. But one approached life as a victim and the other with arrogant pride. Let's not forget, the difference between a journey and an obstacle is attitude. Having a spiritual practice helps you discern the difference.

Our homes and the land they kiss used to serve as a sacred site for seasonal offering. In Andes tradition, the power of their Ti is in direct relation to their offering, or Despacho. Beautiful offerings of grain, seeds, flowers, candy, and other gifts were created and given to thank their God for their home and the earth it stood on. They celebrated her bounty, recognized her healing, and thanked her for caring for their tribe and their crops. By doing such practices, it was a way to recalibrate the Ti, set their world straight, and ask that order prevail over chaos. A practice set forth steeped in gratitude.

In this way, you celebrate all that Mama Earth has given you. You celebrate good fortune and good fate, and see past the artificial notions. When the veil is removed, you can see the growth available from the obstacles, and by doing so, you become one with everything that is beautiful and valuable. Only through ceremony and offering, prayer and generosity can you express the purest, deepest gratitude and touch the primordial light.

Ceremony is not about gaining more stuff, winning more awards, or acquiring more status. It is to show reverence for all that has already been given to you. This becomes a magical act, a form of religious dreaming, and like all great meaningful magic, this is symbolic to Nature and the medicine she provides you. What smart phone can do that for you?

We have lost the art of tradition and honoring our ancestors' deep wisdom. We have lost the art of true gratitude and what it means to be thankful for rain, sun, and sharing a healthy home and meal with those we love. Everything is not as it should be. We have become out of balance with the natural laws, striving for more achievement, wanting, desiring, doing more and acquiring more, rather than being thankful for what is. We are not quiet and peaceful or showing reverence for our greatest gifts, that of nature and all she provides. I encourage you to arrange some stones or flowers inside your home to act as an altar to invite in the forces of the divine and her wisdom. By tapping into your ancestors' wisdom, the divine mind, and the power of nature, you can reveal beauty to a new and original way of being.

To join in ceremony should not be a solitary undertaking. It's about coming together as a family or unit of friends to embrace the higher power, or primordial light. Together, you join hands with the divine to co-create the perfect balance in your life and the lives of those around you. Through community, collaboration, and connection you experience the oneness of all that is. Ask for nothing, give with heartfelt generosity, and express gratitude. This is how you touch the Ti, Prana, Chi, or divine breath and ultimately cultivate the Chi around you.

EXPERIENCING WHERE HEAVEN AND EARTH COLLIDE

The mysterious moment when ordinary elements are transformed into an otherworldly experience is what takes you from everyday chaos to touching the fortunate cosmos. This is the magic of Feng Shui. No matter your faith, these outcomes become your holy sacrament of Heaven on Earth. Practicing Feng Shui brings you in union with God. As you grasp the fundamentals that make up Feng Shui, these mystical experiences will be the outcome of your daily cultivation. Feng Shui is a spiritual practice that has existed for thousands of years. Show it reverence because, like many spiritual traditions, it's not founded only on sacred texts, experiences of others, or on sheer faith and belief. It's founded on personal experience.

I leave it up to you, the student who experiments and plays with the magic to find her own definition through first-hand experience. In this way, you will touch your soul and the divine in your own unique way and feel Heaven and Earth collide.

With that said, it's good to be a skeptic. Don't take my word for the experience you'll have. The truth is "it" is both timeless and infallible. It is through these teachings that our ancestors helped future generations like us expand towards greater consciousness. Due to the doctrine approach that has prevailed for centuries, many have abandoned their belief in mysticism. Religion has become a complete act of faith through devout worship. But to know only one God and one religion is to know none at all. Heaven, divinity, and everything in between is indescribable. It is up to you, the student who practices Feng Shui, or any spirituality for that matter, to find your own inner truths. This is about utilizing a tool that allows you to experience the mysteries of life through first-hand experience instead of reading about it or hearing about it.

Your God does not require any devout worship, but recognition and acceptance through direct experience, generosity, gratitude, and unconditional love. Practicing Feng Shui is to return to yourself and touch your own Ti. To learn who you are at the core, soul level, connecting us, Earth, and Heaven through an altar called home. In this way, you become adept in your knowledge, which distinguishes you from pure devotee to transcending the need for intermediaries.

Like me in those early years of jumping to the good stuff, I failed to recognize the power of Feng Shui to transform my life. And recognition may not come easily. It may require you to go on a mystical journey until you are mature enough to absorb and understand it. It is only through the maturing of the mind and embracing the unknown that you can realize your union with God. This is the ocean you came from and through these tools you can learn to communicate and interpret your relationship to it and learn how to swim. This may take a year, or it may take a lifetime to fully grasp. Nevertheless, God and the mystery that surrounds us is without shape, image, or limitation. This is the ultimate unconceivable force that each of you that reads this book must get to know through your own Feng Shui journey.

INTELLIGENT ENERGY WORK

In order to have your own spiritual experience through Feng Shui, this isn't something that can be rushed. To simply review where a disruptor lies and throw an adjustment will likely prove unsuccessful. For five years, Loho became my petri dish of experimentation and helped me develop The Top Five Disruptors™. She taught me to slow down and really feel into it. She also taught me the importance of doing this work on good days and avoiding the work on bad days. For example, to throw a mirror up to fix your Feng Shui without setting forth your why, and doing it with incoherent Chi, will lack depth and muddle results. To achieve superior Feng Shui results and work on a transcendental level requires a full mind and body connection. It requests that logic and mysticism coexist, science and artistry uniting as one. Ditch what your mind tells you, instead, be guided and open to any and all things that show up. And finally, it requires you to work with energy in an intelligent way. In other words, working without fear, worry or doubt. Only in this way will you wield energy in a powerful and gratifying way, making The Top Five Disruptors™ all you really need to get started on your Feng Shui journey.

5

WIELDING ENERGY

*"Down inside most of us feel that something is missing in our lives and we try
to fill it in all sorts of ways, but only God can fill it. Cultures are different,
people are different, but the needs of the human heart are the same."*
Billy Graham

fter the 2008 crash, all bets were off. Having had three very
successful years in Nashville, I was suddenly faced with a
new kind of Avidya, as many Americans were. This wasn't bad luck,
bad fortune, or even bad karma, this was Maya on a global scale. This
was a blindspot that no one saw coming, at least not the general
public.

*"To everything there is a season, and a time to every purpose under the
heavens."*
Ecclesiastes 3:1

We had become quite gluttonous in our ways as a culture, and this
crisis was our renunciation into what Hindus and Buddhists refer to

as *vairag*, the removing of worldly dust and desires that didn't serve us. As long as non-spiritual matter pulls or pushes us like a belligerent tyrant, we will be unable to find our center, and this is what becomes the void. Striving to find our way through desire, addiction, and excess we lose our identity in egocentric self-indulgence. Our Chi becomes erratic, disease evolves seemingly out of nowhere, and suddenly everything is against us rather than conspiring for us, and we suffer what Buddhists define as *dukkha.*

In order to strengthen your Chi and wield energy in a powerful way, for extraordinary Feng Shui results, you have to become free from attachment and lower frequencies. In order to become free, you have to unlock the chain that preoccupies you to the label that hinders you. For example, labels like the acquisition of more money, achieving more status and power, striving for the perfect body, attaining a bigger house, or owning a better car—these are all empty attachments that promise gratification but are ultimately fruitless and make one suffer. These are shallow desires that do not lead to satisfactory fulfillment, but instead allow the ego to thrive like wildfire.

While the desire may not leave you right away, shedding the need for the label can occur through a rich and complete spiritual practice. With increased wisdom, study, and humility the desire for non-spiritual matter will fall away, and you'll extricate yourself from the material things and seek silence and calm to connect to the divine. Here, you'll discover how it all is and know that we are all connected. This is how you cultivate your Chi and raise your vibration, and this is necessary when doing a mystical practice like Feng Shui.

TRANSMUTING ENERGY

The entire cosmos, in all forms, in every plane, and throughout all dimensions is energy, or Chi. Your body, your home, and the things you surround yourself with are all forms of energy. So are your thoughts and feelings. However, no two forms of energy are treated equally. They differ from one another in terms of the rate of their frequency and vibration. I learned this with my home in Las Vegas.

My vibration, my Chi, was not strong enough to overcome the darkness. The good news is every quantum of energy is synonymous with all other energy, and it's continuously changing, transmuting, and transforming into other forms of energy. Einstein taught us this through the first law of thermodynamics: *Energy can neither be created nor destroyed.* This is what makes everything in the universe interconnected and gives you the ability to change, transmute, and transform your own Chi and become a powerful energy ninja.

When you cultivate your Chi through meditation, spiritual texts, and spiritual teachers, you have the opportunity to communicate with and interact with pure consciousness and the divine matrix. The implications of this are far reaching, as I am implying that the collective is consciousness—something materialist scientists refuse to acknowledge. But when you have succeeded in breaking away from the labels that produce unsatisfactory attachment, you can openly merge with the collective and open yourself to all that is. This is important because what you thought your consciousness was turns out to be a sliver of the whole—remember the bucket of water from the ocean?—and amnesia of the sliver is where the illusion of separateness comes from. When we feel separate, we seek labels to help define us and turn to attachments, addictions, and other external things to fill the void. These are very low frequencies and vibrations, making energy work futile and next to impossible. So, if you've ever placed a Feng Shui adjustment, or done any energy work for that matter, and think it's complete BS because it didn't work, it's likely you're the problem, not the adjustment or energy work.

Although hard for most to achieve, a person who can erase attachments in totality and become one with the whole is said to be in *sat chit ananda,* or truth-consciousness-bliss. This is an existence of total knowledge and pure bliss. This is considered the highest form of samadhi and the highest form of cultivated Chi. Now, your ego may step in and think, *Well I can do that; I just need to set my mind to it.* Once again, this isn't something you can intellectually figure out and make happen. This has to do with your heart, and this occurs in a realm that can't be logically conjured up. The harder you try to think your way through it, the further from *it* you'll go.

Sat Chit Ananda is the highest achieved state of oneness, but short of this state there are many intermediate steps you can take to become free from attachment and spiritual dust to become a powerful energy ninja. What's important to realize is that your being is a conduit through which energy passes. This allows you to receive Chi at a vibration at which you are attuned to. The more you work on your Chi and cultivate a spiritual practice, the stronger and more attuned you'll be to attract potent energy. When you can break your identity with attachment and the labels you think define you, the energy available to you is finer and at a higher vibration; the quality is superior. Imagine being attuned to 110 volts and being upgraded to 220 volts. Here, you'll be able to transform Chi simply by way of thoughts, voice, and body, better known as the mind, body, speech connection. In other words, when you break your attachment to the physical plane, you free yourself up to the vibrational energies that are more subtle and finer but far more powerful. Bottom line, unless the electrical fixture—your body—is suitably adapted, you can't tap into the higher, more powerful energy. And if you live in a house like my Las Vegas house was, you'll find it difficult to wield and transmute Chi in a capable way. Again, it's not that the adjustment isn't working, it's that your instrument isn't fine tuned and working at a state that can handle it. It's great that you got a new washer but only if you have the ability to plug it in and use it! Following are tools that will help you plug in.

MINDSET

It's imperative that you create a new framework of habits and way of thinking. If you don't have the life you want, then you require a new way of thinking, a new mindset. Avoid filling up on non-spiritual matter, and instead look to activities that spiritually cultivate you. Spending time in nature, doing spiritual workshops, reading books, and meditating are great places to start. However, don't try to maintain your current habits and dabble in spiritual matter. Trying to walk both paths simultaneously can be dangerous and can create new karma or even new attachments, which will lead to the loss of attuning to the higher energies.

It is necessary to acknowledge where you are in your development, and start there. Denial or trying to race to the finish line will get you nowhere, but will instead feed the burning fire of the ego. Besides, you have no idea what the finish line is, what it looks like, or how to even get there. Hell, it may not even exist! Mindset cultivation is the only way to know the answers, and cultivation comes only through time and work. Your only goal is to work with the energy for the highest good, to turn everything you do into one of love, and compassion. When you glimpse through the veil, and experience something extraordinary, then you've transmuted the energy. In the beginning, this may be difficult to achieve. You may only glimpse "it" for a moment. It may occur over a matter of moments. What's important to note is that you'll have moments of bliss and moments of shear disappointment. Every bit is divine work, even if some days you have to see profanity as sacred. Accept your limitations, remove all shame, judgement, expectation, and guilt and do everything you can to transmute the energy in a positive, and more importantly, fun way. And if you can't do it today, tomorrow's a new day! Hallelujah!

WE NEED NEW THINKING

In addition to changing ones mindset, it's also necessary to change ones way of thinking. Our rational mind, the instrument that assumes we can think our way through everything, has been coarsely tuned and awarded in our culture as the supreme great power. Originally used as the primary source for our survival, in modern times it grants us increased pleasures, feeds desires to the point of excess, and awards us with status and power. These measures all enhance the ego by seemingly mastering control of our environment. Simultaneously, as we feed this demon with great voracity, we miss the horror that convenient urban living has done to our planet. War and killing now makes most numb, runaway imbalances in global ecology make most feel powerless, and inequality in economics has left most hopeless. This leads me to believe that our rational mind and the adage of 'business as usual' has led us astray.

"A new type of thinking is essential if mankind is to survive and move towards higher levels."
Albert Einstein

The rational mind can only take us so far, and it's time we move past the patriarchal pollution of rampant egoic ways. We need to transcend this way of thinking, go in a new way, use a different vehicle, and come back to our great ocean of consciousness. This illusion of separateness has been fed by our current system far too long, fueling competition, and a dog-eat-dog world. This has caused an increase in addictions like gambling, gaming, shopping, drugs, and pornography, and some don't make it out alive. The suicide rate has increased exponentially because people cannot withstand the pressure or the loneliness. And knowing fully where we go when we die, I can't say I blame them.

Now, I'm not saying we throw this amazing tool out with the bathwater. We first need to explore how we can utilize this tool in a healthier, more positive way. That is, can we figure out a way to use this mind to transcend itself? Can it get out of its own way? I do think it's possible. Through positive spiritual matter, we can arrive at intelligent reasoning but only through discrimination and discernment. Only then we can build a better vehicle that serves us.

Ultimately, we have a choice. We can use the great power of the mind to lead us to freedom, or we can continue into greater enslavement. To fully understand the risks, if we can see it as that, we must first recognize our limitations. The current paradigm is that we are all separate. Our database is based on what's known through stereotypes, parental and societal conditioning, and the experience of our limited five senses lodged into our memory. Here, we find old imprints from childhood that we aren't worthy, not good enough, not pretty enough, not smart enough, wealthy enough, and so on—and these challenge our *true* essence. Fear, judgement, shame, and other Below the Cross Emotions set in, and we are forever in the loop of lack and fear. Thus, we turn to the acquisition of more goods, more status, addiction, and excess to lick our wounds, stuff our feelings aside, in hopes to fill the void through coping. Ah, the American way!

I'm not asking you to close all accounts with reality. You do, however, need to change your way of thinking. Lifting the veil to see your attachments and what they truly mean to you is to look fear square in the eyes. To fully accept that you are a divine, omniscient being with more power than you know will help you to understand the fundamental truth of what you are capable of when doing energy work. Attachment to labels and things are what hold you back. It's what keeps you caught in the illusion of separateness. Only with study, discrimination, spiritual work, and discernment will you transcend this worldly illusion that you think is real and arrive to the transcendence we all have access to.

We can think and talk about this way of being, but how does this help your Feng Shui results? Why does all of this matter? Many of us are afraid to let go of our discerning, intellectual, and judging minds. To do so could mean imminent death! Once again, this isn't something you can think your way out of; this is something that is felt through your heart. This has to do with the mind-body connection to tap into realms you can't even fathom, and this is available to you through opening the heart.

Your heart is your direct line to God. Through it, you can experience emotion, which is a built in barometer straight to whether something is good or not so good. This is how you experience *home*. Unfortunately, we've been conditioned to have a stiff upper lip and ignore this great gift. Get past the stereotype and you'll experience a tidal wave of love so intense from the divine, it will carry you beyond your way of thinking to a way of just being. This is where those finer, subtler energies reside. So you may be saying, *How do I do this?* One way to start experiencing this devotion is through *kirtan*, or communal chanting. In many ways, chanting a mantra is like chanting mystical poetry that opens the heart. If you're new to mantra, kirtan allows you to experience it, and to explore it in a community setting like a yoga studio. Opening your heart to love is totally safe, no matter how scary it may seem, because the object of love you feel is ultimately reconnecting to your true self. This is how you start to overcome the ignorance, or Avidya, and start rising to your own *sat chit ananda*.

POWER OF INTENTION

Intention and visualization are key ingredients in Feng Shui. Through intention you can activate your adjustment or ceremony with powerful blessings and remedy an issue. This is where having cultivated Chi and a powerful mindset become essential. Combined with mantra, you create a mind, body, speech, connection that becomes a very potent tool for the conscious mind to produce sacred transcendental change. The more specific you can be, the more grounded you can become and the better your results will transform you. And don't allow modest intentions to step in. Oftentimes we think small, feeling guilty for asking for too much. If you're asking to change something in your life that you believe will truly better your life, then it is believed to be sincere and in your highest good. If your intention is pure to your heart and in line with your vibration, you will wield energy in an effective way. Black Sect Feng Shui is derived from the philosophy of Tibetan Buddhism. Its main objective is to alleviate suffering, or *dukkha,* of all sentient beings, and that includes you. Through this beautiful art and cultivation, you can learn how to better your life and improve your circumstances through the power of intention. We didn't come to Earth to mindlessly recreate existing lifestyles, jobs, or ways of thinking. As souls, we came here with the gift to create! But many of us have not been taught this or have forgotten our true nature. Feng Shui allows you to play with your innate abilities and takes you from a place of stagnation to ultimate creation.

CAN WE ALL JUST HAVE A MYSTICAL *SOULU*TION?

In Feng Shui, there are two approaches to finding a solution to energy vices: mundane or transcendental. Both are seen as equally important. However, both are vastly different.

Much of our lives is approached with logic. If we can make sense of it, figure it out, and conclude the *why*, this is considered within our range of experience and explanation, better known in Chinese as *Ru-shr*. Rational, sensible design solutions are types of solutions that are considered acceptable and reasonable because they stem from our base of known knowledge. They incorporate common sense and sound judgement as a way to accomplish your intentions. An ideology of, "we've been here, done that, and know the outcome." This makes it safe and acceptable.

Let's take for example someone looking to find love. A mundane solution may be to get out of the house and perhaps socialize some more. Or maybe take a class where you know others have a similar interest, or maybe you join a dating service. These are practical solutions to solve your desire for love. However, these types of solutions, while very important, may only yield ten percent success. Remember, in Chapter 3, we discussed the five key factors that make up Feng Shui, and there are many things beyond your understanding that factor into the outcome. These variables stem from karma, luck, and fate. As we become more enlightened with positive spiritual matter in our lives, we can start to see that our lives are not as clear as we'd like to think. It involves an intricate cobweb that's contingent on many different moving parts. That's why we want to employ Feng Shui methods to problem solve in a more open-minded and productive way.

When we move beyond the mundane and practical approach, we arrive at what's called transcendental. This type of solution is far more mystical, illogical, irrational, and beyond the realm of known knowledge. This is known as *Chu-sr*. This is a solution that lays beyond our realm of experience and is very mystical in nature and often cannot be explained. These are the solutions that are met with criticism and pessimism because they suggest remedies to a problem that appear absurd to our highly intellectual way of reasoning. Let's revisit the request for someone looking to find love. A transcendental approach may be to place a mirror at the foot of your bed because it helps you move forward and increases self-esteem. It's also a beautiful balance of yin and yang, creating harmony within the bedroom. The positive outcome of applying a transcendental *soul*ution can yield an outcome that is believed to be 120 percent more effective. Not only does it resolve the problem, it also simultaneously enriches your life with spiritual matter!

Playing in the mystical nature of Feng Shui is still a mystery to me, even after twenty-plus years of practice. Its mundane aspects align well with physics and science, but its transcendental approach is far reaching and encompasses a large expanse into the unknown—what is yet to be proven, discovered, or even understood.

Ultimately, the way I see it, is if you told me to stand on my head naked and sing show tunes and it would bring me the love of my life, the promotion, infinite health, or happier children, I'd do it. I don't need to understand it; I just need it to work. Transcendental Feng Shui allows you to attain a desirable end result by increasing Chi in your life in a positive way that's very mystical in nature and unexplainable. If you need logical explanation, I can't provide it, but the whole purpose of Feng Shui is when the environment is improved, your Chi is improved, and you attract more health, wealth, and happiness. Let the naked show tunes begin!

HOW TO WIELD ENERGY

When working with Feng Shui, it may be tempting to ignore the mundane altogether and go straight for the transcendental adjustment. Ah, look at you getting caught up in logical thinking! It would seem reasonable to go straight for the higher outcome probability. Why accept ten percent when you can have far more? The mundane, however, is equally important when utilized with the transcendental option. Remember, there are many variables at play for which you don't fully understand, nor do you have control over. I encourage you to practice all mundane solutions, in addition to applying the transcendental improvements. Consider for a moment that the transcendental adjustment needs a vehicle for which to show up. It needs a tangible situation through which to manifest itself in your life. If, for example, we return to our example of wanting to find love, the mirror *soul*ution will increase your self-esteem and help you to move forward, but the mundane solution of getting out of the house affords you access to align to the energy of your new mate. She/he is not going to conveniently show up in your closet. Trust me; I've tried.

I think it's safe to say that you have the mundane part of life down. If not, you're reading the wrong book. In order to wield energy in an omnipotent way, many things need to occur. You need to create a lot of positive spiritual energy to do purification work, or transcendental work, and your current habits likely won't get you there. You cannot reside in the dense physical plane, full of negative emotions and attachments, and expect miraculous events to occur. The energies, the frequencies don't match. The good news is you have the power to change, transmute, and transform energy. Yes, you! By changing your mindset to one of fostering growth, setting clear intentions and fine tuning your instrument through positive spiritual practices, you're well on your way to enlightenment. *Ohhmmmmmmm.*

One of the easiest and productive ways to shift mindset and vibration is through meditation. It is a crucial means to achieving higher states of awareness like compassion, higher truths and selflessness. One of the greatest questions in Buddhism is, *"How can we create conditions for happiness? How can we eliminate suffering?"* This is one of the reasons to practice *dharma*, or universal truth. To transform one's spirit, to change one's being and way of thinking is understanding the universal truths to reduce negative emotions such as attachment and aversion. To practice dharma is to reach for nirvana.

According to the Dali Lama, *"That which spurs real change in your spirit is meditation."* Meditation is mental training that results in a calm and luminous mind. In Buddhist tradition, meditation posture takes great importance. It is believed that, in order to develop mental calm, your spine must be straight. The legs are crossed in a diamond lotus position, the chin slightly lowered, eyes closed, and the tongue softly against the top palette of the mouth. Relax your shoulders, and place hands in your lap, the left palm on top of the right with the thumbs touching. Breathing calmly in and out. The legs, hands, posture, mouth, head, eyes, shoulders, and breathing are the eight elements of *vairocana*. Continued practice of *vairocana* will relax the mind, help you achieve extraordinary clarity, and even clairvoyant abilities can occur!

For many people, meditation is hard because all they know is *doing*, rather than *being*. But, in order to achieve an extraordinary life, you cannot force anything, nor can you logically figure a way around it. You simply have to do the work. Meditation not only calms the mind, it calms the spirit, the Chi, and smooths it out. Smooth, balanced Chi will allow your transcendental, mystical experience to unfold, and this is one way to wield energy in a dynamic and powerful way. But we will learn more about this in the next chapter.

MIND, BODY, SPEECH

In Feng Shui, intention and imagination are emphasized through a tool called the Three Secret Reinforcement. It's a way to reinforce your intention in the physical plane to achieve a desired spiritual result. This is where the integration of mundane and transcendental, or outer and inner form, define successful Feng Shui. This is a sacred ritual that adds influence to your adjustment and seals the deal. It's an active physical blessing ritual that combines three mystical, sacred ingredients: the mind, body, and speech connection. Utilizing this ritual expresses your intention, and empowers your Feng Shui blessings in an active, meditative state. It's a way of expressing your mind through intention and visualization, body through a prayer mudra, and your speech through mantra or prayer. This brings the completeness of your being into the act of the mystical, connecting the physical planes to the spiritual. In doing this, you prepare your mind and body to receive your deepest desires, and align with blessings that bring you closer to enlightenment. Using this reinforcement empowers you and your Feng Shui and seals the desire with intent. In other terms, you're telling that energy what you want it to do and where to go! Haphazardly slapping up a mirror or crystal will be in vain if you don't tell it what to do. It's essentially like getting in a car and expecting it to drive itself without having the keys to make it run.

THE FENG SHUI TOOL BOX

There are several basic remedies that are used in Feng Shui to alter, diffuse, moderate, or raise Chi. Used for both interior and exterior uses, these remedies resolve imbalances and improve the flow of positive Chi. The essence of an adjustment is based on just that, its essence. Oftentimes my clients will think that a small adjustment can't possibly heal something that physically seems huge. This methodology spotlights using something that logically seems too small to achieve or overcome something quite large. For example, placing a small, faceted crystal to reshape a missing area of your home. But keep in mind, the strength comes from its transcendental reinforcement. This is where the cultivation of your Chi comes into play and brings the transcendental power to your object. And that transcendental power can move mountains! Otherwise, an object is simply an object. There are many things that we use as practitioners to push, pull, diffuse, relieve, absorb, radiate, and protect our environments. The following list is by no means complete but a great place to start. In essence, these items are merely mundane objects until you address what the item's purpose is, and you infuse it with transcendental Chi. Take the time to take care of your Chi. The more cultivated you are, the more powerful and sacred your mundane object becomes.

Bells and Chimes - This is probably one of my most favorite adjustments, and my clients will tell you, I always recommend bells and chimes at the front entrance. Chimes radiate sound in a ubiquitous way and are incredibly uplifting. They adjust the flow of Chi by diffusing and softening the impact of a road, or road noise. On a front door, they can stir and lift Chi. They disperse Chi by redirecting it and tempering it in a more beneficial way. Plus, you can use them to call in positive Chi, like new opportunities. When hung on all four eaves, they can lift the Chi of an entire home. Most importantly, if using any kind of chime or bell, it should be made of metal and the sound it produces should be a throaty and enjoyable sound.

Color - Yet another favorite, as an interior designer, this is how I create designs that are Energy Aligned™. In Feng Shui, color is a powerful conduit to enhance one's life in both a mundane and transcendental way. Color is vital to our overall health and well-being, but when combined with the power of the Five Element Theory, like the constructive or destructive cycle, or the rainbow spectrum, you attain a full system for positive change. Individual colors may also be chosen to enhance one's Chi. For example, all white spaces are incredibly popular in interior design, but this creates a lot of the Metal element. If you are a dominant Wood element, you likely will not feel comfortable in an all-white space over time because metal chops wood. You may become depleted! The solution would be to bring in the water element of black to water your wood, or more green for vitality.

Crystals - This tool is prevalent and most widely recognized and associated with Feng Shui. These multifaceted, round crystals adjust Chi flow by resolving imbalances and enhancing energy in a positive way. Since they act as refractors of light in all directions, they have the ability to alter imbalanced Chi that shows up in a negative way. In addition, they become symbolic of positive change, reinforcing your intention every time you see it.

Lights - These are considered a staple in Feng Shui to enhance our environment. Used both outside and inside, lights can fill in a missing piece and reshape your home. They can hold Chi in, connect Chi and enrich an interior with its symbology to the sun. In general, lights are a way to improve our environments by brightening them. Through their potential to bring illumination, lights are a terrific solution to stir and fire up Chi. For example, a bright light that turns on automatically at a front door that is small can increase opportunity and thinking, not to mention increases the feeling of more space.

Living Objects - Anyone who has pets can agree, they stir up Chi.

Not only in their actions, but also in how they influence our personal Chi. Other living objects like plants and flowers are also great ways to boost Chi. They not only symbolize nature and growth but also nourish and encourage Chi. It is believed that when a plant thrives, so will its residents. Not only do plants benefit us and make us happy, but they can also resolve imbalances that can harm our Chi, like acute knife-edges. Another option is flowers. Although short lived, flowers have an astounding effect on our mood, elevating our Chi. I think everyone can attest that receiving beautiful flowers immediately boosts and excites her Chi!

Using any type of living thing is a way of capturing their life force to add benefit and vitality to your environment. Plants, animals, fish, and even trees all adjust Chi. This book would not be complete if I did not give reverence to my love affair with trees and nature. Not only do trees harbor great wisdom and strength into our lives, they act as powerful guardians. Through trees, what many mystics consider to be the first land shamans, we touch Heaven and Earth. Through their deep roots, they connect us to the underworld, grace us with their presence through the earthly realm, and reach for the sky, bridging us to the heaven realm. Large, old trees, what are called the grand-mothers and grandfathers, are especially sacred. Many people have special connections with trees, a feeling they can't deny or explain.

Trees act as powerful protectors. They can screen against all sorts of negative influences, like exterior knife-edges, ominous buildings, roadways, and traffic. Strong, healthy trees indicate excellent earth Chi and highlight vibrant Chi of an area. If you enter a subdivision or area where many trees are struggling, this is considered an omen of bad earth Chi.

While most trees are considered beneficial, in some cases they can hinder good Feng Shui. For example, a tree that blocks a front door by feeling too close. If it feels oppressive, it's not beneficial. A dead or dying tree at the entrance is especially bad. This can indicate a loss of resources, or portend bad luck or a death in the family. If a tree must be trimmed, pruned, or cut down, *always* do a ceremony and honor them with reverence.

Mirrors - Mirrors adjust a bevy of interior and exterior ailments in Feng Shui, making them the aspirin that heals many woes. Amongst a mirror's many uses, through intention, they can control, push, absorb, expand Chi, counteract negative issues, eliminate a bad influence, and improve Chi by showing off a beautiful view or drawing in resources like flowing water. If your entrance is small or narrow, a mirror can expand the Chi.

Moving Objects - Adding moving objects in and around your home is a great way to stir Chi. Recently, I recommended a client place wind chimes and a moving garden sculpture at the entrance to her home. Not only does it deflect oncoming traffic and soften Chi, it has elevated her Chi with pure delight every time the wind blows! Windsocks, kites, moving sculptures, and flags are all great ways to activate, lift, and stir Chi.

DON'T WASTE WATER IN THE DESERT OF MATERIALISM

If you take anything away from this chapter, I hope what sinks in the most is revamping your daily habits, because it matters when it comes to your Chi. The tools listed in the Feng Shui toolbox, while powerful and necessary to shift Chi, are rudimentary in nature without a calibrated and wise captain. Take care of your personal Chi and cultivate it daily. Change the way you think, behave, and act. Be mindful and intentional in all that you do, otherwise wielding energy will be a fruitless act. It is not your time, your effort, your money, or any material goods that have value; in fact, they have none. It is your karma that you leave with that is most valuable. Only through kindness and compassion and what you give to others will you gain great change and good karma. These are energies for which you can transform, transmute, and transcend in a prolific way. And these are energies that will give your Feng Shui tool box the notes to compose a beautiful symphony of positivity and change.

Undertaking any major change like this will most often be met with resistance and fear. Change is scary! Breaking habits can be arduous! Materialism and consumerism has seeped into the lives of many as a way of being. In *Dying to Wake Up*, Dr. Rajiv Parti shares that his materialism not only defined him but it became who he was as a human—that is, until he was diagnosed with prostate cancer. For two grueling years, he endured chronic pain, dependency to pain medications, depression, and seven surgeries. The last surgery, as told in his book, he almost didn't survive. With a fever of 105 degrees, as his wife raced him to Cedars-Sinai Hospital, sepsis and severe pelvic infection were setting in. As he was being prepared for surgery, his consciousness separated from his body, and Dr. Parti began having a near-death experience. From above his body, he experienced the stench of his infection, watched as doctors raced to save him, and then he floated further beyond to experience a heavenly realm.

Despite Spirit telling him he had become gluttonous and materialistic, he struggled to let go of it all. Who was he without all this stuff? Who was he if he wasn't a prominent anesthesiologist with the most prestigious home and a garage full of cars? Even after communicating with the heavenly realm and being told to change, he still met it with resistance. The ego is a faithful servant!

Luckily, after Dr. Parti's experience, his behavioral and psychological priorities changed. In the weeks after his surgery, he left his prestigious career, and with the support of his wife and children, they downsized from their ten thousand square foot home to a modest family home. He traded in his fancy cars for a practical hybrid, and now he volunteers and spends time teaching others that chronic pain, addiction, and depression are "diseases of the soul." In a radical departure from his conventional medical training, Dr. Parti now advocates a consciousness-based approach to healing. Bravo!

I'm not asking you to ditch your lifestyle like Dr. Parti did, although it may be necessary to untether your ego from the shallows of material ways. You have to ask yourself what's truly holding you back and harnessing you to non-spiritual matter. What will be necessary to create authentic, meaningful change in your life? Listen, looking at life in this way is frightening, because it's different and against the norm of what culture tells you is acceptable. For most, it's against all things we've been taught are acceptable. Change sparks fear. It awakens the goblins within the ego. Here, we come face to face with pride, judgement, and self-pity. We resist change for a number of reasons, but mainly it's because it's overwhelming, too hard, and seems meaningless. Change can also be confusing, and the discomfort of time dragging on makes us feel like it's happening too slow. As a society, we love to rush and do for the sake of doing, and who has time to wait and cultivate? We want the instant gratification of arriving at the other side, *now*. These are all demons of the ego, booby traps placed to foil your plans, disguised as pain so you hurry back to your safe, old ways. If you let it, it will succeed a thousand and one times. But if you are true to your own soul—ready, willing and able— you will succeed! You will fall and fall again. Hell, I've been at this for over twenty years, and I still fall. The swiftness with which I turn things around, however, is much quicker than before. So you just get back up and try again. Desire will knock on your door again and again and again. If you succumb, let it go and get on with it. Just accept where you are, don't fight it, don't punish yourself, and remember, tomorrow is a brand new day! Cue the choir!

Each of the elements listed in this chapter are here to help you raise your Chi. If taken seriously and diligently, the effects, even with a modest approach, will manifest into more calmness, mindfulness, and happiness in your life.

The things in your life do not define you, but they will anchor your energy and prevent you from aligning to your own *sat chit ananda*. When it comes to Feng Shui, you are your greatest weapon for change. When it comes to your soul you are the master of your own fate—so choose wisely.

6

THE IMPORTANCE OF PRAYER AND DEVOTION

"Prayer is the daily recognition of the unseen and the eternal; this is our inevitable duty to honor the essence of all things and this can only be strengthened through spiritual devotion."

Wisdom of Native Americans, Kent Nerburn

In 2009, I was experiencing a lot of pain in my abdomen. One early winter morning, I was in so much discomfort that as soon as I pulled up to my design firm, I headed straight for the back corner where my office was to unbutton my pants. The pain got so severe I started wearing yoga pants to work, and even the elastic band would cause discomfort. Finally, when it got warm enough, I started wearing caftans to work, but I was faced with yet another dilemma when my undergarments started causing issues!

After the 2008 crash, a new kind of fear had set in, one of lack and scarcity. Well-established clients eager to furnish their whole homes had dried up and contracts were being broken left and right. I went from having a year's worth of work to nothing in a matter of months.

At the time, my overhead was close to $20,000 a month. I didn't have time to worry about my pain. I was young, took care of myself, and I had a much bigger issues to worry about, like the fate of my firm! In addition to my career falling apart, cracks were starting to appear in my marriage. I was desperately trying to revive my trifling spiritual practice, but it would get thwarted by my spouse interrupting my meditation practice with judgement and mockery. I had turned our guest bedroom into my sacred place, secretly hiding all my devotional tools—hiding as if I'd be burned at the stake—and pretending it was my reading room. Here, I could meditate, journal, and contemplate how to make sense of it all. Mainly, it became a place to completely freak out and conjure up worst-case scenarios on a daily basis.

This is a moment in time when my faith in God and the esoteric was not one of purity and truth. Nor is it a shining example of trust and belief. To be honest, I wavered on whether to include this section in the book. I'd always been true to my path, full of love, compassion, and faith, and here I had succumbed to the very thing I feared: the faithful servant, the ego. I was beaten down by the trials and tribulations going on around me, desperately trying to control everything and hold on by a thread. I begged and pleaded to be saved from it all. If this energy stuff was real, if there truly was a divine, supreme system, I demanded to be freed. As we well know, it doesn't work this way, and while I would be freed from it all, things were about to get real messy over the next five years.

NEXT STOP, CANCER

My firm's future was hanging in the balance, my marriage was on the rocks, and soon I was about to get a diagnosis that would catapult me into who I am today. I had been putting the doctor's appointment off for months because my husband had lost his job, and we didn't have health insurance. After weeks of no sleep in the spring of 2009, I started making really big mistakes. One such mistake was when I arrived at my office early one morning to find the door wide open. I had left the night before without any of my belongings and never bothered to lock the door. People I knew for years would come by the office, and I would just stare at them blankly trying to place how I knew them. The last straw was when I lost my new iPhone and found it two days later resting at the bottom of a cup full of water in my car's cup holder. *How did it get there? Was I even in my car? Wait, what day is it?* What made this situation worse is that my spouse was not supporting me. He had completely checked out, and it felt like we were living separate lives. I would get beaten up all day at the office struggling to find work, and then come home to an apathetic and aloof partner.

When I finally went to the doctor, I already knew what was coming. Months earlier during a deep meditation, I had heard, "The chains that bind you will be unearthed." I knew that my foundation was about to be rocked, and I knew something big in my life was about to occur because I kept having dreams of standing on a treacherous cliff. Despite all this, I still tried to control, rather than surrender. Two weeks after my doctor's appointment, I was called back in. When I asked why I needed to come back in, the doctor said there were some inconsistencies and nothing to worry about. She lied. That was code for, "We have really bad news and we don't want to tell you over the phone."

When the nurse escorted me to the back of the doctor's office, she placed me in one of the rooms and, as she left, she looked at me with the most sympathetic eyes. The fear felt like a fire racing through my body, and I began to sweat. I could hear my heartbeat in my ears and throughout my head. When the doctor finally came in, I couldn't even muster words out of my voice. It was like the TV channel inside my head was whizzing faster and faster through each channel, and words became muttering nonsense. She opened the file and finally spoke.

"We got your test results back. You have stage 4 ovarian cancer. We need to get you into surgery as quickly as possible, but I will need to get this scheduled with a colleague of mine who is an oncologist. He's in Chicago and specializes in this type of cancer. It has consumed your entire pelvic area, and we will need to do a complete hysterectomy. I've had success in the past, but yours is aggressive. I would recommend you get your affairs in order, just in case."

She placed her hand on mine, gave it a soft squeeze and walked out. Despite getting the worst news of my life, an overwhelming sense of calm came over me. I'd like to say it was the divine, but I think it's safe to say it was delusion. That is, until I got out to the parking lot and called my mom, who's a registered nurse. I told her what the doctor told me, and I shared the test results. There were three or four tests done, including the CA 125. Typically, this test shows markers around 50-75 that indicate that cancer is likely. My test results came back at 575. Combined with the CT scan that verified a mass the size of two footballs in my abdomen, cancer was not only likely but confirmed, in my mom's professional opinion.

Mom got on the next flight out to Nashville. She seemed extremely worried about this diagnosis, as if she knew something I didn't. Delusion was turning into shock, and I was afraid I didn't have my wits about me. I felt guilty, but I called into my office and told my staff I wouldn't be making it in. Honestly, I'm not even sure how I made the twenty-minute drive home, and I would soon regret the decision to skip work.

When I arrived home my husband was standing in the kitchen getting ready to leave for the gym. He asked why I was home and I told him I was just diagnosed with stage 4 cancer. I'll never forget the next words out of his mouth.

"Why are you being so dramatic? Everyone survives cancer these days."

He set his cup in the sink, grabbed his keys, and left for the gym. I was still in shock, but maybe he was right. Maybe I was just over reacting. I opened up my computer and started doing research on my prognosis and discovered my mom did know something I didn't; many women did not come out of this alive.

OVERCOMING DESPAIR

Too often, people hear their results and become the prognosis. When my mom arrived in Nashville, she dragged me to four more doctors to get a second, third, and fourth opinion. They all landed on the same target. But I kept hearing the words from my meditation, "The chains that bind you will be unearthed." Deep down inside of me, I knew that the only way to overcome despair was to return to my spiritual practice. Only through spiritual matter would I find my way back home; yet another reason Marlene had been brought into my life so many years before. She brought me home back then and would do it again.

Before Marlene had passed away, she had told me about an amazing woman named Linda, who lived in Fair Oaks, California. She was a medical intuitive. I had never worked with someone like her, and I wasn't entirely sure what it entailed, but my soul was guiding me. When I called Linda and told her about my diagnosis, she surprised me by asking why I had manifested it. *Ummm, what?* She went on to describe the subtle energies that surround our body. When all those energies are in harmony, your body flourishes; you're strong and healthy. When there is stress in your environment that you refuse to address, disease manifests. It starts to appear in subtle energies, what's often picked up by a traditional Chinese Doctor as an imbalance in an element or meridian. Unfortunately, those subtleties in our Western culture are often ignored. Only when the body manifests a sizable symptom can it be addressed in the Western world. Oh my God, I had sick Chi.

What I came to realize is that, if I was going to fully connect with my roots of universal intelligence and who I was at a soul level, I would have to go all in. I couldn't treat the symptom that I had manifested. Sure, I could have the surgery, but what I needed to evaluate is why I got it in the first place. I knew that if I put my energetic system back together in a more harmonious way, I would create that perfect yin yang balance and become whole again. Only when in balance would my soul flourish and have fertile soil in which to bloom. I had not cared for, nurtured, or honored the soil necessary to fully bloom. I had ignored it, shoved it down, and lost myself in the illusion.

With Linda's guidance, I began a devout spiritual practice again and did it with reckless abandon. I didn't care who saw or what they thought, because at this point I had nothing to lose. My guest room officially became my church, a truly sacred space for healing from the inside out. Meditation became a twice daily practice. Mantra and prayer were filled with gratitude, not demands. I incorporated an hour of silence into every day, built a devotional altar, and studied ancient texts like my beloved Tao de Ching. Eating was treated with respect and prayer and sleep would become my body's altar to marinate in my daily healing activities.

In December of 2009, just before Christmas, I had my surgery. Not only had the cancer shrunk, but the surgeons discovered that the entire mass had moved to my left ovary. Rather than having a full hysterectomy I was able to walk away with one missing part.

When I woke up from my surgery, my doctor was dumbfounded, and all she could say was, "It's a miracle."

When I told her what I had done she just smiled and said, "It's always good to pray." *Eye roll.*

"I don't believe in magic," the young boy said. The old man replied, "You will when you see her."
Atticus

This milestone solidified my belief in magic and miracles. It also cemented the importance of prayer and devotion in my life. Several years later, other than a foretelling scar, you'd never know I was ever diagnosed with cancer. In fact, few people even realize I went through it. When they learn about it, they are shocked, and I realized more people need to know that they too have the power to wield their own energy system back into one of health and well-being. Healing is an inside job. Whether you work on your own Chi, a loved one's, or that of your environment, it's all one and the same. Fear, shame, doubt—all those Below the Cross emotions are toxic soup for the soul, and it will prevent you from ever creating healthy vibrant Chi if you allow the ego to thrive. If you're not healthy, neither is your environment. It is an intrinsic, delicate cobweb that requires constant recalibration, commitment, and devotion. This was my final gift from Loho before I moved out. She reminded me that my energy work matters. In those final days before my surgery, my prayer room became an incubator for health and healing, and I have her to thank for giving me that space to bring me back home.

IN THE NAME OF GOD

Humans have always tried to categorize and compartmentalize the many powers of Heaven. We've even tried to identity *it* with labels and inherent qualities like male or female. Perhaps this is for the ego to recognize its very existence. For example, the divine feminine, being expressed in the forms of The Virgin Mary, Mother Nature, and even goddesses like Venus or Kali. Or male counterparts like Jesus, Muhammad, or Shiva. It's as if God has to separate into several different aspects, or be compartmentalized, in order for us to embrace it and acknowledge its power. Only once it's named and given a purpose can we invoke it and comprehend it. Boy, do we love to over-think things!

Whatever it looks like for you, your spiritual practice is geared to awaken your divine potential, revive your soul and cultivate your Chi. Spiritual matter liberates you from your physical limitations and spotlights your infinite potential. God, or whatever the name you give *it*, helps you to shed light on your own darkness, reveal the little-known corners of your soul, and illuminate your brilliance and divine light. You are incredibly powerful, and you have strengths that you have yet to awaken. Your devotion is a source of emotional, physical, and spiritual influence that helps you free yourself from fear so you can develop an aspect of personal empowerment and rise above the illusion. Your fears versus your strengths is what divide your spirit into polarizing duality, making faith and doubt wage an eternal battle deep in your psyche. It's time to consolidate the faces of your spirit and bring its true power back into daily life so that you can mindfully direct your thoughts and actions into one of love and compassion. Routine devotion is what helps you to act honorably and intentionally, helping you to see your almighty power and live up to your divine potential. Unfortunately, we've been led to believe and conditioned to think that we are less than. When we go against our true essence, our true divinity, disease, unhappiness, and suffering abound.

YOUR DIVINE POTENTIAL

Choice is your greatest weapon, and you have the choice to choose a different path. Some may argue it's too late. But here's the thing: no matter how long you've gone in the wrong direction, you have *the choice* at any given moment to turn around. The experiences and relationships you are meant to have are in your life to support your spiritual path and overall growth. Indeed, every interaction and experience is an opportunity for you to grow and transform into who you are meant to be. This is your ultimate divine potential. Some relationships will be sweet and empowering; others will feel like pure suffering. Each is an opportunity to exercise your wisdom in whether to see it as part of the journey or succumb to it as an ordeal. Take for example someone apologizing to you for realizing they spoke to you in a hurtful way. In that very instance, you have a choice: the power to transform that energy to one of compassion or you can catapult it to the density of rage. Obviously, transmuting it to one of forgiveness and compassion instantly turns that transaction into an exchange that restores and empowers. The choice is yours. Most choose to hold a grudge repressing their divine nature which causes divine potential to become a contaminated transaction. Choosing to act in accordance to your divine potential is the only way to bring the internal and external world to one of love, and the only way to reach ultimate contentment. In other words, it's never too late to turn it around.

Your divine potential, when calibrated through a spiritual practice, is the fullest expression of your natural spirit. Only in this essence can you discover the depths of your full soul capacity to create, express

FENG SHUI FOR THE SOUL

love, give compassion, show forgiveness, and be generous. More importantly, your divine potential becomes clearer and clearer when you let go of the need to know everything, and just let be. It becomes less important as you realize that it's all a part of the Maya. And don't be fooled. Your potential will never be revealed to you all at once. Your unrealized potential will be the motivating force that drives you to find the meaning of life, and the Maya is coyly placed there to try to foil your plans along the way.

Like a hero on a mythic journey, you are meant to confront struggle, be faced with crossroads, and figure out the path. Your potential asks you to rise above the ego and reach for your highest self. And you cannot grow only by using your intellect. Divine law and logic are vastly different, especially when viewed through the lens of the ego and its accompanying immature emotions. You will be ambushed, face decoys, and step on many landmines along the way, but through a spiritual lens, you can navigate with maturity and find the deeper truths.

Your practice will guide you into a realm of symbolic perspective, and the more you practice, the more you can dramatically make better choices. When your life plan suddenly gets interrupted, you can choose to view it as a spiritual modification to revise your current path, or you can see it as a crisis. You have a choice: it can be viewed as an antagonist foiling your egoic plans or as a blessing from the divine showing you your greatest strength and potential. Choose wisely.

SPIRITUAL PRACTICE 101: ALL THAT'S POSSIBLE NOT PLAUSIBLE

To truly tap into your divine potential and wield energy in a commanding and potent way, you cannot lack faith. To go on this journey with despondency and skepticism will land you right back to where you are, forever in a mind-numbing loop of sameness. The greatest travesty in our modern-day culture has been the loss of faith in the unseen. When mysticism is genuinely embraced, your life opens up in unimaginable ways.

Several weeks ago while in yoga, my teacher had a dharma talk around Saint Dunstan, the patron saint of all blacksmiths. In folklore, it is said that Saint Dunstan is known for safeguarding himself and others from the devil. Enamored by his skill and ability to turn away desire, the devil portrayed himself in many ways, even a beautiful woman, to woo Saint Dunstan from his craft. Finally, Saint Dunstan took his blacksmith tongs, struck the devil on his nose, and threw a pair of horseshoes on his hooves. In great pain, the devil screeched and demanded that Saint Dunstan remove the shoes.

"Only on one condition," replied Saint Dunstan. "You must never again bother another blacksmith, and you can never enter a home that bears a horseshoe over its door."

Because of this act of compassion for others Dunstan was awarded sainthood, and anyone who placed a horseshoe over their door was provided protection from the devil.

I love stories like this, and it is my belief that each story of folklore has a thread of validity to it. What I found disappointing is that, as I did more research on this story, it was met with skepticism and disrespect. As adults, we have become so jaded by the Maya, or illusion of it all, that we've lost our faith and childlike wonder to the mysteries of this world.

If you plan to do this work and expect to get 120 percent results, you're gonna have to believe in the work. When I got my diagnosis, I could have easily slipped into mind-numbing sameness. I could have become my prognosis and succumbed to fear. I could have allowed that disease to consume my body and play the consummate victim. Instead, I chose faith. With Linda's help, I saw my divine potential for all that was possible not plausible. That means putting logic and pessimism aside. Through your faith, clear intention, and ceremony, ordinary objects will become extraordinary talismans of transformation.

As Henry Ford so famously said, *"If you think you can, or you think you can't, you're right!"*

CREATING A SACRED SPACE FOR SPIRITUAL PRACTICE

In my earlier years, one of the biggest struggles I had was creating a sacred space that *felt* truly sacred. Originally, I started out in a closet, then I moved into the guest bedroom. It held a pitiful nightstand left over from college and a possessed lamp that worked when it felt like it. Even though it didn't feel like it, or look like it, every bit of what I did in these spaces was divine work. Because what you think it should be like or look like is the ego showing up with her devilish expectations. You can argue that creating a space to conjure up worst-case scenarios isn't exactly divine work, but it did eventually lead me to burn out and get to what matters most: a spiritual practice that got me back to myself again. If that's not sacred, I don't know what is!

If you are steeped in Below the Cross Emotions, change directions for a moment and wonder, "What if?" Imagination is the fastest way to epiphany and dramatically helps you get out of your own way. Too often, we default to the lack, fear, and scarcity that seemingly surrounds us rather than hold space and bear witness to the true essence of Self. What if, instead of dwelling on all the things that are going wrong, you focused on all the things going right? And what if you visualized the things going right manifesting into more amazing things going right to be grateful for? A spiritual practice is a positive daily ritual that puts you back in touch with who you truly are. It clears your mind of clutter that does not serve you, and reflects back to you your natural spirit. Through a spiritual practice, you get glimpse's of that spiritual ocean you came from and see your own light.

Most of us are embroiled in the world moving around us, and we easily get swept up in nontrivial things. We can overthink everything to the point of being paralyzed, and then do nothing. This isn't about creating the most beautiful space that you think it should look like, or having an entire space devoted to your practice. Simply taking thirty minutes at the kitchen table, or sofa, to read a beautiful spiritual passage, journal about its meaning, and then closing your eyes to quiet the mind is enough. It is every bit as sacred; it is every bit divine.

In the beginning, be kind with yourself and try different methods. What works for one person may not work for you. More importantly, look to each method as a way to opening you up to a new way of being. My yoga teacher has said many times to imagine a full lotus flower as the ultimate goal of enlightenment, and each time you learn something new, you've gained a new petal on your flower. Get in touch with who you are, remove the worldly dust that weighs you down, and learn to see yourself as you truly are: a beautiful divine being made from love. Whether you attain enlightenment today, in a year, or perhaps your next lifetime doesn't matter. It's the journey to becoming a more loving and compassionate person that is your most important task of the day. Don't get trapped in your expectations. A spiritual practice can show up as yet another obstacle if you become too attached to its outcome. Take the time necessary to allow your petals to grow and fully bloom.

Traditionally, to have a place of meaningful worship and ceremony within your home, one should have an altar. Whether this is in a small corner, a closet, or an entire room dedicated to devotion is up to you. By setting up an altar, you create a space that initiates devotion and worship, encourages meditation and prayer, stimulates you to read spiritual texts, and strengthens mantra and reflection. An altar holds space and grounds you to your spiritual practice. It builds a strong center. This is a place that reminds you to get in touch with yourself and see yourself as a part of the great ocean. This is also an excellent place for ritual by making offerings of love and gratitude through grains, incense, flowers, candies, feathers, crystals, or whatever else feels noteworthy to you, to that which is holy to you.

Make this space simple, special, and pure. This area can become sacred to you through intention. Have a chair or meditation cushion to sit on, light candles or incense, and before you start your devotion, visit your altar and make a beautiful offering to show reverence. You may wish to include beautiful statues of deities on your altar that have meaning to you, like Jesus, Buddha, Allah, Goddesses, or whatever is important to you. Not only do holy statues add beauty and sacredness, but also photos of loved ones you wish to bless or help who are suffering or sick is also a great addition. Opening yourself to this love and compassion opens your heart and brings your loved ones to the light. Keep spiritual texts on or near your altar to include before or after your practice to add to your daily spiritual fruit.

If you already have an altar, consider expanding it. In my opinion, more is more! You can never have too many spiritual places within your home to deepen your spiritual practice. This is how you allow Spirit to permeate every area of your life and alleviate you from *dhukka*, or suffering. Surround yourself with the divine to remind you what is most important in life. You can even expand your holy space into the garden with holy sculptures, crystals, bells, and lanterns. Create a temple that spiritualizes your life from the inside out.

MEDITATION

The art of meditation is letting down your defenses and just being rather than doing. If you allow it, meditation will be your greatest gift to yourself. I will often tell people that I am not an intuitive, and yet I can't tell you how many times I will be sitting in meditation and get "downloads." Over the years, one of the greatest gifts meditation has given me is insight and clarity into my clients' lives and their homes' needs. Before every consultation, I spend two to three hours in a meditative state. I walk in nature, I write, I read, and I meditate. I fill my morning with spiritual matter. When clients want their appointment moved to the morning, I refuse, because it messes with my process, and it messes with their messages.

Personally, I have learned that discernment is key, and I may not always understand the message, but it needs to be told. Earlier this year, I was working with a woman who had recently gone through a divorce and was not looking for a relationship. While in meditation, I very clearly received that a new fling was coming into her life and this fling was imperative for her next chapter in life to unfold. I almost didn't tell her, until I confirmed with her astrologer and her reiki practitioner that indeed, love was coming! Over the years, I have received many important insights like this for my clients, but none are as important as the ones directly from their homes. As I was writing this book, my meditations were filled with visualizations to propel this book to the masses, that everyone learn to add spiritual matter in their lives and cultivate their souls through Feng Shui. One day, deep in my own visualization, in popped a house, her name was Lola. I knew exactly who she belonged to.

"I need you to let her know that I need a note," she told me.

I tried to make sense of this request. Within my thoughts I replied, "I don't understand. A note for what?"

"That I am loved, that they love me. I need a note and it needs to be where everyone sees it."

Then she suddenly started shaking my shoulders back and forth as if to peacock her pride and shake her stuff. She was as ecstatic as a three-year old getting a pony.

When I saw the homeowner a few hours later in my office, I let her know that her home's essence had visited me, and that she needed to give her a love letter.

No surprise, the home owner just smiled and said, "Do you know what happened yesterday? We finished the front of the house. We removed the plywood and all I kept saying was, 'Oh, my God. She's so beautiful!'"

It never ceases to amaze me how connected this intricate cobweb is. This is the magic of having spiritual matter in your life. If you are still, you can resonate with the silence between the notes and understand the vernacular of your home and environment. This is sacred space. Your home is a part of you, intrinsically connected, and if you love on them, it shows. If you listen to them they speak. Don't underestimate the language of home. Through meditation, you can hear her whispers, and if you pay attention, you'll realize that she's always communicating with you.

Cultivating a meditation practice allows you to emanate a spiritual resonance that reverberates throughout your home. Hold gratitude for her, express love, and connect with her like the family member she is. No amount of pretty can create a space that feeds the soul like love, devotion, and admiration can, and no amount of pretty can create love that is truly recognized like sacred space can.

Keep a journal with you while in your sacred space. I like to call them *Gratitude and Grateful for, Joy Journals.* A journal does not need to be a lengthy, drawn out process. Somedays I write one to three sentences of all the good in my life, right now. Other days, I write three pages. Sometimes I skip it all together. A journal helps you to reflect on your thoughts and actions. It also gives you a way to process and record the gifts you receive from meditation. Only through recording and documenting can you recalibrate yourself back to equanimity. In addition, I encourage you to keep your journaling positive. At the end of this chapter is an excellent exercise on Joy Journaling to help you get started.

Meditation is simply a tool for quieting the mind. Some will argue that they cannot meditate. I disagree. Honesty with yourself about where you are and learning how to overcome your "addiction to busy" is what will help you to be okay with stillness and get over the excuses. It's not that you can't meditate, it's that you don't know how to be still. Meditation is a tool that gets you out of the "doing" and gets you to a place of deep listening and "being." It is a tool that intensifies insights, peels away the layers that aren't real, and brings you to a place of tranquility.

A consistent meditation practice can be quite eye-opening. It shows you the egoic dust you've built up and how that defines your external, universal reality. Without a spiritual practice, the ego will keep you busy in an endless story of nonsense full of desire, expectation, fear, and judgment. Through regular practice, you can dissolve the ego's power. I encourage you to do it even when you don't feel like it. You will constantly be berated with other desires. *I wonder what's happening on social media!? I should post about last nights dinner!* But that is the faithful servant stepping in to tantalize you with empty calories. Practicing regularly helps you see how your ego imposes limitation, lack, and fear and falsely colors your true existence.

Practice with joy and appreciation. Do not enter into it as one more thing you *have* to do. The idea is that it leaves you so full that you are constantly hungry for more. As you do it, your awareness is going to wander, and you'll be attacked by stray thoughts; just allow them to be. Don't try to change it, just notice them. The easiest thing to do is simply focus on your breath. "I'm breathing in. I'm breathing out." You can also use the mantra, *So Hum*, which means I am that. As you breathe in, *So*, as you breathe out, *Hum*.

To start, after you've made an offering at your altar with clear intent, sit comfortably with your body as straight as is comfortable. If you can, cross your legs in the lotus position on a cushion. If this is not possible for you, sit in a chair. Take two or three slow, intentional deep breaths just to get grounded and centered. Focus on your breath. In and out. Another tool that can be useful is to use a *Mala*, or set of prayer beads. *Malas* are a way to keep count of your mantra or breath. They are intentionally made with 108 beads. The number 108 is sacred in many Eastern religions including Buddhism, Hinduism, and Jainism. In Tibetan Buddhism, *Malas* are usually 108 beads plus the guru bead to reflect the words of the Buddha or *Kangyur* which has 108 volumes. The number 108 is also sacred because it is a complete system, holding space for the number one all the way through nine, which we come to when we add the one and eight together.

The art of meditation is to allow. The thoughts will come, and you will initially get fidgety. Don't get upset or feel like you are doing it wrong. Very gently, again, and again, and again, simply bring your awareness back to your mantra or breathing, and keep at it. Use prayer beads to help you to focus. As you become more practiced you'll crave the time with yourself and miss it if you don't do it. And the more you do it the calmer and more intuitive you'll become.

"Meditation is the highest form of prayer. In it you are so close to God that you don't need to say a thing. It's just great to be together."
Swami Chetananda

PRAYER MANTRA

There are many paths that can lead you to a more enlightened aware-ness. Some, like meditation, will feel like an uphill battle; others will be generous and kind. For many, meditation feels like an uphill trek filled with dangerous quagmires. *How do I find the time? How do I still my chaotic mind? Why am I not receiving profound information like others? Has my back always hurt this much?*

You will notice that the more people you meet doing meditation, the more you will find them singing its praises because it's a method that has worked for them. They are getting a return on their time and effort and gaining greater knowledge. The trap is that you strive to attain what *they* have, and what *they* are getting. If you are not feeling this experience, and getting such a return it can break your level of devotion as something they do, not what you do. But as one does this, it exposes the finiteness of expanding your current reality, which cannot be done without a tool. The quagmires may overwhelm you, but this too shall pass, if you give it time to unfold. Searching and seeking for other methods that can yield the same kind of outcome is just conning yourself. That searching will ultimately become a short-term strategy at best, and leaving you filled with negative emotions at worst, because meditation is the best way to find your equanimity.

To safeguard against defeat, many teachers recommend a mantra. One of the greatest obstacles we face in meditation is our own thoughts. Thoughts are what keep us stuck in the forever revolving ego of sameness and separateness. And no matter how hard you try, those thoughts just keep coming. Guess what. Those thoughts are all a part of the illusion. Your goal is to transcend your individual bucket and return to your ocean. In order to do this, the immediate goal in meditation is to quiet the mind. *How on Earth do I do that,* you say? Through chanting a mantra. This is how you reach the depth of your being. As mentioned, *So Hum* is one of my favorites for beginners!

Essentially a repeated prayer, passage, affirmation, or holy deity name is a mantra. The intention is to state your mantra again and again and again like a continuous loop to concentrate the mind. This helps you to get out of the ego mind and bring you back to the *I am*. It brings you right back to the center of the heart and to the *now*. It can be recited out loud or silently, any time, any place, all geared to protect the mind. It protects you from going into its usual mechanical, habitual behavior, which skews your perception of reality.

Think of your mind as a lake of rough water. What you seek lies deep below, but as you try to see beyond the surface, choppy waves and water whisk by. Those waves can show up as expectations and obligations. Your boat violently rocks from side to side, making it harder and harder to see past the illusions. Thoughts whip from all directions: old memories, today's to-do list, the calls, the emails, routines and habits—all running on autopilot without a kill switch.

Now imagine a new way of being. Smooth water, no waves, and complete stillness. *Ahhhhh.* The obstacle known as the mind becomes calm via a single thought that collects the mind, and this is a mantra. Now, an even level of thought coming from one direction overrides your choppy waves to one of deep, still water. Each ripple in the water is the same, and no other thought can intrude or grab your attention.

I've seen it said that still water can be regarded as stagnant, dirty, or inactive of life. On the contrary, in Feng Shui, we do not see a body of calm water as stagnant and lifeless, but a representation of our intelligence and our deep wisdom. Only through depth of knowledge can you find good judgement. The deeper the water, the greater your intelligence and the wiser your judgement will be. If you continue to stay in the shallows or on the shores of your meditation practice, you will never reach your fullest potential and never see past the illusion of separateness. The shallower the water, the fewer opportunities that come to you. Only through practice, dedication, and time can you tap into your higher intelligence and deep wisdom.

You may ask yourself, *Why is it necessary to break from my thoughts? I like my thoughts!* It's necessary to break the label associated with thought so you achieve inner freedom from the ego. Will thoughts still come? Yep. Thoughts will continue, as it's a natural process, but now you will identify them as separate from you, rather than feeling like you have to attend to them right away. Now it is simply realized and let go, and you gently return to your mantra.

Many mantras used in meditation are in Sanskrit. I've been asked by my own students what the meaning of the mantras are and if they can recite them in English, and the answer is no. Sanskrit is the root of the Indo-Aryan languages of which English is derived from. This language was created consciously, meaning each sound syllable resonates to a specific sound that correlates to a specific energy center, or chakra. Thus, the meaning of the mantra and the sound of the mantra are its purity, its essence, and its healing. As told by my own teacher, Katherine, who worked under H.H. Grandmaster Lin Yun,

> *"Trying to translate a Sanskrit mantra allows words to get in the way. Out of respect we will not translate a mantra. We keep it as it was given to us. We no longer speak Sanskrit so it would be very difficult to translate it and do a good job. It's the vibration we want in our heart and mind. Translation can twist the words around and its full meaning and essence lost. Mistakes and omissions can be made, therefore we keep them in their original form. The important thing to remember about mantras is their vibration, not understanding their translation."*

In addition, many mantras used in meditation are given by teachers. Is this necessary, you may ask, for it to work? Not necessarily, but being given a mantra ensures its meaning as it is passed from teacher to student. Reading something online or in a book can be less effective and less powerful because it lacks connection to our ancestors. This is a spiritual passing of energy that, when you receive it and recite it, it's so deep within you that you touch that same spirit. Whether a student who grabs one from a book or off the Internet encounters this same essence of power will depend upon her level of faith she brings to it. If she brings little faith or commitment to it, then she will encounter little return. But if she brings to it great faith, she will get the highest returns. Many teachers who pass on sacred mantras do so only when they know the student is ready.

Having sufficient faith in the power of a mantra and its spiritual nature is the only way to use it. Coming to a mantra with other means where the student does not have faith and hopes it to perform will fall short because she will be unable to intelligently transmute the negative energy she holds, and she is not mature enough to understand why.

HOPE VS FAITH IN YOUR SPIRITUAL PRACTICE

When you have a spiritual practice, you are in touch and in tune with God through the power of devout faith. But as adults, we can cloud this connection with cynicism and fear, and get stuck in this dense physical plane of busyness. Children, on the other hand, innately have this connection and don't question it. They are not worried about tomorrow and certainly don't dwell on the past. It's all about the right now. Furthermore, children don't misconstrue the difference between hope and faith. They simply trust in all that is, and they can teach us a thing or two about hope and faith.

Hope is what anchors you to lack through a lens of deservingness, *i.e.* I hope that I get the job, get pregnant, find the love of my life. Hope still embodies a level of fear and worry that it won't come to be because of something else. Your ego attaches you to all the mistakes you've made and all the fears of the future that could happen, making you waiver in absolute belief. Faith, on the other hand, is what frees you to all that is through God's love, *i.e.* I will get the job, I will get pregnant, I will find the love of my life because I trust that it is in my highest good. That is true faith through absolute trust in God.

The importance of prayer, meditation, and devotion in your life reminds you daily to always hold faith. To trust in all that is and that you are always taken care of no matter the illusion. When you lose that connection, that belief to trust, hope sets in and can quickly turn to sadness and despair. You lose your partnership to all that is and see yourself as separate. This can allow the chaos of the physical plane to set in and consume you. I was recently reminded of this myself when my friend, Amy Stark, shared a story of her son taking her from a place of hope and rooting her into a place of faith. A great reminder of how our children can be great teachers.

> "Recently my son and I were with friends and their children at a very crowded, chaotic setting. All of a sudden one of the children who was two and half years old, disappeared. All of the parents began to panic, including myself. My son looked at me and said, 'I can't see him mom, but I can sense him, and he's ok!' I realized he was right, so I looked at him and said, 'You're right little dude! Let's do this.' And off we went using our greatest gift, our energy and our faith.
>
> "Our children can be our greatest teachers and they remind us of what we already know, but forget amongst the chaos. I was in fight or flight mode and he was in empowerment mode. Empowerment is always the place to be in."

They found the two-and-a-half-year old shortly after, not because they hoped they would but because they had faith they could. When you drop into your mechanical habits, you lose your conscious perspective. The more you practice and cultivate your devotion, the easier it will be to ditch the hope and gain empowerment by means of unlimited faith. Fame and money will never give you a sense of permanent depth or achievement, and that's why developing faith and trust through prayer, meditation, and devotion is the most valuable currency there is. It provides the gateway to eternal spiritual achievement.

SILENCE

In our modern world, silence can show up as a bevy of objections that need to be orchestrated, scheduled, and fiercely controlled, a time that you should desperately try to carve out for yourself, but likely rarely seek. If you achieve the time to find silence, most rush to fill the gaps manifesting more frenetic energy because silence is so foreign. To hone a spiritual practice, silence is necessary for quiet reflection and contemplation, and yet most have not fully grasped its importance. In fact, many fear it. Few of us are skilled in beholding all that is in the sacredness of silence. Mainly because we have been so heavily influenced by the noise and busyness of our current world and its seeming expectations. An article written by Rasha Ali in USA Today called, *Social Media's Obsession With Work is a Job Itself*, states the following,

"The glorification of always being occupied with work is tied into our self worth." The article finishes with photographer Samia Minnicks stating, "People have a problem with stillness. It creates this sense of anxiety. A lot of people try to stay busy to avoid what comes with stillness."

In the midst of so many activities, we have lost the priority, beauty, and necessity of disciplining ourselves to behold prayer and devotion within the space of silence. Yes, most of us are busy, but everyone should narrow their lives down to what is most important through silence. The Bible says that we must be still in order to know God. Isn't it interesting that the very thing we need to bring ourselves to center is the very thing we run from? Silence is a necessary act of devotion if you really want to know and reconnect to all that is. It is one of the greatest disciplines you can give yourself to smooth out your Chi and quiet the mind.

You may be saying to yourself, *Why the hell do I* want *to be silent? I like my crazy-busy world!* #nevernotworking

We all manage and cope with stress differently, but to practice silence is to manifest more clarity of mind, calmness, and most importantly, it teaches you the enhanced ability to listen. Too often we talk at each other, only to hurry up and tell the person how their story relates or how it reminded them of something else. No one ever listens anymore, too distracted by the trivial things we call life. I can't tell you how many times I am in a conversation with someone who interrupts me, talks over me, or doesn't listen. It is truly becoming a lost art. I see it showing up on radio shows, TV shows, and podcasts too. I am told all the time how wonderful my podcasts are and how insightful my questions are, and it's because I am truly listening to what my guest has to say and giving them a platform for which they can speak their truth without interruption—a rarity in this day and age.

The purpose of silence is to exercise and develop your inner witness. Through clarity of mind, you can notice how you interpret the reality around you and discern with better judgment what is truth. I encourage all of you to take time each week for silence. I practice silence often and my greatest insights, truths, and wisdom come from it, like the evolution of this book. Let your family know, and ask for their support in your weekly endeavor. Use a chalkboard, whiteboard, or piece of paper to write anything that needs to be said at that time. The beauty in silence is it teaches you to get to the point!

Another way to practice silence is to get up thirty minutes earlier in the morning. The morning holds such sacred space for clarity, and it embodies the calm before the storm. If you aren't a morning person, utilize the time in your car in between appointments or on the way to work to practice silence. Turn off the radio and simply drive in silence. In fact, many activities can be carried out in silence. Gardening, cleaning, driving, cooking, writing, knitting, whatever it is, gift yourself with weekly acts of silence. This trains the inner witness to see how your mind has the propensity to run away from you. Time not spent doing busy can be spent fulfilling the assignment of inner work. Busy for the sake of busy has limited value in helping you break through the illusion.

CONSCIOUS EATING

Cooking and eating should be a sacred, spiritual experience. Silence and prayer is a way to return to God; eating is how you come in holy contact with God. Through the act of deliberate and intentional cooking, you make a conscious effort to heal from the inside out. The entire process of cooking is one of ministry. From choosing your meal plan, to selecting delicious, beautiful fruits and vegetables, to chopping, prepping and cooking—this act should be like church going down in your kitchen. Through food, you treat your body as the temple it is and fill it with the very things that God created, like sun, plants, and earth.

Your constitution, your very make up, is where you live, work, and become enlightened every day. No different than external environments that are more conducive to spiritual matter, your body itself needs to be treated with respect and purified too. What you eat affects your temple, but how you prepare affects its vibration. What enters your body can either support you or deplete you. Choose wisely.

To best prepare your temple for optimal Chi, consume less and eat healthy, conscious foods. This may seem like common sense, however there is a *why*. Earlier in Chapter 5, I discussed how to wield energy in a powerful way. Much like Below the Cross Emotions are dense and heavy, so are poor quality foods. Heavy starches, red meat, and processed foods can negatively affect your energy system. In addition, to really get into the energy of it all, processed foods contain very negative vibrations in them. Take for example the palm oil ingredient. I spoke about palm oil in my 2018 book, *Easy Everyday Habits to be More Eco-Friendly*. The $40 billion palm oil industry is notorious for wiping out rainforests, displacing indigenous peoples, spewing more carbon into the atmosphere in one day than the entire U.S. economy, and driving the orangutans, tigers, elephants, and entire ecosystems toward extinction—all for more profit. This one ingredient is literally tied to the energy of indifference and greed. Not to mention, enormous sadness as the fear, anxiety, and panic those animals felt before their imminent death is left behind on the land and in the soil. You may try to argue that the residual energy cannot possibly be left behind, but I can tell you from first-hand experience, I have been in places that experienced rage, anger, hopelessness, fear, and anxiety, and I can just as easily slip into that energy today and *feel* it as if it just happened. There is no energy as strong as that of trauma. And my Las Vegas house, Goldie, is a great example!

When you consume food, you take on that food's Chi, or energy. Be mindful of the vibrations associated with the food and the vibrations you drive into the process of prepping, cooking, and eating your food. This is one of the reasons that many spiritual beings do not eat meat. Any food that entails violence or harm to the planet can be invoked with fear, anger, rage, and other Below the Cross Emotions. Animals have a consciousness, and they experience fear knowing their fate. Before being slaughtered, they release adrenaline and other chemicals into their bloodstream, which in turn goes into the meat. This can greatly affect your energy system and your ability to elevate yourself to higher states. Recognize and be conscious of where your food comes from. I'm not saying you have to stop being a carnivore if that's your thing, but perhaps take into consideration getting your meat from a local farmer who treats his animals with kindness and humanity. Two entirely different energies, indeed.

Food that entails prepping, chopping and cooking should be invoked with prayer, love and mantra. The only state of mind in which to prepare and eat a meal is calmness. There is a wonderful Sufi saying that drives this theory home:

"If a person eats with anger, his food turns to poison."

In my own home, not only do I chant while I cook, but I am notorious for delighting in my food's beauty. I often tell my fruits and vegetables how gorgeous they are. I delight in their colors, their sweetness, their beauty. I've shamelessly posted such admiration on social media sharing my delights. Rushing to throw a meal together or repeating a toxic thought in your head while you cook is not being conscious. That is the ego holding you to the past or fearing the future. Instead, choose to be present and grateful. Consecrate every part of your meal, and make it a family affair. Listen to music, laugh and drive joy into the entire process. Food that is loved with pure heart will pour into your soul with absolute joy.

Always bless your food. This is how you awaken your truth, hold gratitude and set forth intention. Be thankful for all that is and all that you have. To delight in a healthy meal brings you in direct contact with God. Whether it's a bowl of cereal or a feast, thank the farmers, the factory workers, and all the hands that touched this food, including God's, in order for you to have this meal. This brings you into contact with all that is and the oneness of all there is. And if you are out at a restaurant, be mindful of all those coming into contact with your meal before it arrives. Use this time to hold space for gratitude, or chant a mantra, say a prayer. It doesn't have to be a big production, but it can become your living connection to the divine and a way to raise its vibration. *Thank you* is one of the highest forms of prayer.

SLEEP: MARINATING IN YOUR HEALING

In a society that glorifies busy for the sake of being busy, many people sacrifice sleep as a way to gain more time in their hectic day. To me, sleep is such a necessary human need to perform my best, and yet our Western culture treats it as a low fruit commodity. What's more interesting is that I see culture, whether it be through articles, TV or movies, idolize the idea of working all the time in an effort to be important and in demand. You're either climbing your way up or maintaining what you've built, and both demand less sleep and more time. But have you ever asked yourself why? Because most are chasing a fictitious carrot that does not exist.

"You're spending money you don't have for things you don't need to impress people you don't like."
Walter Slezak, Keeping up with the Joneses, 1956.

In college, I would stay up late in an effort to study before a big test. I would cram all night, then in the morning gulp down a Mountain Dew and a glazed donut and get the grade. But this is not intelligent or sustainable. And thus after college, I never did it again.

One such fictional character that embodies this excess culture was Jeremy Piven's character, Ari Gold, from the show Entourage:

"Don't waste time worrying about work/life balance or looking for your best self, sham 'secrets,' or any other snake oil being pushed by sloppy hippies who have never built a business, let alone a bankroll. Or you will wake up twenty years from now poor, pissed off, and primed for a midlife crisis."
Ari Gold (fictional character played by Jeremy Piven.)

Ari's pace in the show would lead any human straight into a mid life crisis, drug addiction, and heart attack by the age of forty. I think the greatest travesty or snake oil we've been fed is the need to work harder and sleep less in an effort to consume more, have more, and be more.

In the West, we tend to fill our lives full of non-spiritual matter, become workaholics, then cry wolf about being too busy and lack time. And we wonder why our health takes a toll and our bodies *betray* us. If you ask most people about their day, it's likely filled to the max with several hours of social media, YouTube videos, Netflix, and email. Not to mention the time-consuming addictions we waste on pornography, shopping, gaming, eating, or gambling that seemingly help us cope. Our circuits are literally being interrupted constantly and then what little sleep we do get becomes impossible, turning into insomnia because our fragile energy system can't turn off. In order to focus, Cal Newport states the following in his book, *Deep Work*:

> *"If you keep interrupting your evening to check and respond to e-mail, or put aside a few hours after dinner to catch up on an approaching deadline, you're robbing your directed attention centers of the uninterrupted rest they need for restoration. Even if these work dashes consume only a small amount of time, they prevent you from reaching the levels of deeper relaxation in which attention restoration can occur. Only the confidence that you're done with work until the next day can convince your brain to downshift to the level where it can begin to recharge for the next day to follow. Put another way, trying to squeeze a little more work out of your evenings might reduce your effectiveness the next day enough that you end up getting less done than if you had instead respected a shutdown."*

The goal is to bring your demanding schedule back into one of harmony. Perhaps instead of working more to make more, to attain more, you choose to eliminate the empty calories. Is playing video games for four hours every night really adding value to your life? Is the twenty hours a week on Facebook contributing to your health and well-being? The more spiritual matter you add to your life, the less you need the external activity and stimulation to fill it. Perhaps this would be a good time to read, meditate, reflect, write, or take a walk. Just imagine what that could do for your circadian rhythms.

My friends often laugh at me at how I live my life. But like all things, it is a choice, and we all have the right to choose. For example, I haven't had TV in years. You may say to yourself, but how do you stay informed?! I don't, and that's the point. I don't need to know about the wars, the violence, or the devastation. I don't need to know how appalling our President is or isn't. And I certainly don't need to know what a Kardashian wore to the Grammys.

What I do need to know is how I can benefit this world with my energy. How can I utilize my own primordial light and gift it to those who need healing? How can I teach people that they, too, have light within them; they've only forgotten? That is my most important task of the day, and that can only be done through rest and reflection, not worry, distress, or distraction.

I challenge you to add spiritual matter into your daily activities. Whether it's an empowering podcast on your way to work, a good book in the evening, or prayer and meditation before you go to sleep. Without spiritual matter in your life, it is easy to lose your way in what matters most. It is easy to get caught in the hustle of illusion driven by the ego. Sleep is your personal health altar that brings you back to yourself and that can only be achieved by *being*, not *doing*. It allows you to marinate, regroup, and recuperate to be your best self. And only in this way will you be able to truly serve with a full cup.

THE OCEAN OF LOVING AWARENESS

The importance of prayer and devotion is to become aware of the divine and your role within it. Take away the ego and the humanness of it all and we are simply divine spiritual beings from a vast ocean of loving awareness. In order to raise your vibration and tap into your ocean of loving awareness, you have to live fully in each moment. There is no past; there is no future. There is only right now.

Our mind is a flagrant wanderer that constantly needs to be

reminded of what truly is. Using these practices daily will teach you how to be more present, open your heart, and bring you back to your self. A devout spiritual practice is designed to bring spiritual matter into your life and bring you back in touch with your true nature. This is the only way you can see the reflection of spirit within yourself and rise above the illusion of it all. These daily practices allow you to add divinity and sacredness in all that you do. Whether at work, taking the kids to school, or running errands, it is every bit sacred and divine. Without an anchor to the spiritual world, we can easily forget and get stuck in the grind of life.

We lose what truly matters. Following daily rituals will become a beneficial habit that allows you to add spiritual matter in everything you do. It's a reminder each day of how you may have gotten lost, taken a wrong turn, and how you have the ability to readjust the navigation and get back on track. Each day is a new opportunity to get back to yourself. Your spiritual practice is not a way to achieve more, make more or do more. This is to help you get in touch with who you already are but may have forgotten. Whether this happens today, in ten years, or when you die doesn't matter. Start today, and awaken to the possibility that the universe is within you. All you have to do is recognize it.

EXERCISE

JOY JOURNALING

Gratitude and Grateful for...

Each day, either first thing in the morning or before you go to sleep, write down at least three things you are grateful for in a few short sentences. The trick to this exercise is to include gratitude for things you already have, but also include something you don't yet have in the physical form. For example, I'm grateful for my job, my family, and the silverware in my kitchen. But I'm so very thankful for the meaningful relationship I have with my mother-in-law.

1. What do you do for living? Do you love your work? Share your gratitude. Do you wish for something that feeds your soul? Tell the universe how grateful you are for all the new opportunities coming into your life.
2. Do you feel blessed by your family? Share your gratitude. Do you wish to have a family? A stronger family dynamic, or have more peace? Share your gratitude and envision

family contentment and allow the universe to welcome it into your life.

3. Has your spirituality grown? Share your gratitude. Are you grateful for your ability to connect with God in new ways? Or would you like more ways to connect and wish to expand it more? Share your gratitude and invite in the possibility of more.

4. How are your relationships? Are they strong and fulfilling? Are they supportive? Share your gratitude. Would you like a deeper relationship or perhaps a meaningful relationship in your life? Share your gratitude and discover how the universe provides.

5. Have you been fortunate to have impeccable health? Are you fortunate to enjoy delicious healthy foods and take care of your body with healthy habits? Share your gratitude. Would you like to achieve better health or healthier habits? Share your gratitude and allow the universe to show you how.

TAKING COMMAND

"The real voyage of discovery consists not in the seeking of new lands but seeing with new eyes."
Marcel Proust

From the spring of 2010 to the summer of 2013, my life was chaotic, extremely stressful, and very challenging. After surviving my cancer diagnosis, I thought I had surpassed the worst, but little did I know, it was just the first crack of the avalanche. My beloved cat of eleven years became ill and suddenly died, I moved six times, fell into severe debt, was forced to close my retail design firm, filed for divorce, and just when I thought I couldn't take any more, the debt collectors started harassing me. I was $30,000 in debt, and my Chi was so erratic and chaotic, it was nearly impossible to work. It's extremely important to understand that just because you have spiritual matter in your life, it doesn't mean life becomes devoid of challenge and sacrifice. But what it does give you is strength and courage to move forward if you dig deep into your soul of experiences to find a way out. It can empower you, albeit on shaky legs and broken voice, if you choose to step back and see the bigger picture and glean understanding from a higher wisdom. Is it easy? Hell no. These were the hardest years of my life, and some days profanity, anger, and sadness had to be seen as sacred.

Looking back, I see the enormous growth I had during this time. These years ended up catapulting me into the person I am today, but it felt like an iron being heated to a thousand degrees on a daily basis. It was the closest I've ever been to hell. I learned to focus on the Now moment, because it was the only way to survive. At any given moment, I was dealing with so much stress that if I glimpsed to the past or took a peek at the future, I'd spiral into despair. I conditioned myself to focus only on what was in front of me. From moment to moment, I would inch my way through the day. I also learned a new form of gratitude. (The joy journal from the previous chapter is what I used.) To be thankful for every little damn thing, no matter how small it was. Kindness from a stranger, nature, taking a yoga class, having a fork to eat my food—to me it was all precious. It's important to mention that society has been built in a way where humans haven't been given space to grieve or heal. It has been encouraged for millennia to push down emotions, ignore them, and "buck up." Any one of my experiences during this time could have been considered a life altering event: cancer, death, loss of a career, divorce, and bankruptcy. For three years, I held my breath, taking shallow sips of air, trying to get through each day, certain another shoe was going to drop. Despite the anxiety, I pushed forward. I had bills to pay and responsibilities to uphold. I lost thirty pounds during this timeframe from stress and inability to buy food. I had no one to count on but myself, so just keep moving forward, I told myself. How I felt and my trivial emotions were hazardous to my future, so I ignored them.

My final straw occurred in the summer of 2012. At the time, I was a part of a networking group that I desperately hoped would help me kickstart my broken career. And, side note, 'desperate' is the wrong kind of Chi to attract anything! It started every Tuesday at 7 AM. We would all meet at a local coffee shop and take turns going around the table selling our craft, and then we would ask for what we needed help with that week. On a Tuesday, in late August, Jane the real estate agent asked for us to give money to a gal at her church.

As Jane put it, "She's going through a nasty divorce, has nothing, and she was forced to move back home until she can get back on her feet." Jane continued, "Even if you can offer twenty or fifty bucks, it would be helpful."

At that moment, I thought of myself. *Wait, I'm going through the same exact thing. Why isn't anyone helping me? And I don't have family to live with!* Then to my horror, the cash envelope was handed to me. Everyone was looking at me to put something in it. I handed it to Dave the architect and said I needed to run to my car. I was enraged, sad, humiliated, angry, and disappointed. Not only did I not have anyone to help me, but I didn't have $20 to my name. I was on the verge of having my car repossessed and had negative $2 in my bank account. When I went back into the coffee shop Jane came running up to me.

"Here's the envelope" she said with delighted fervor.

I quietly muttered, "Oh I'm sorry Jane I don't have any cash on me."

Without skipping a beat she said, "Oh, that's ok. Just write me a check."

Two weeks later Jane was still hounding me for the $20. I finally had to tell her I didn't have the money. Her face went from joyous delight to completely perplexed.

"What do you mean you don't have the money?" She laughed out loud. "Everyone has $20 to help another person out! Stop being a tight-ass and just give me $20. It's the right thing to do!"

For the first time in my life I felt shame. Unbeknownst to me, Jane had taken my power. I was humiliated beyond imagination and my solar plexus, an energy center known as the "gut feeling" area, felt like it was going to explode. Up to this point I had been holding it together, but the dam was breaking and I had officially hit rock bottom. And I knew if I didn't stop taking shallow sips of air, I was going to have a heart attack by the time I was forty.

REACHING A STATE OF EQUANIMITY

When it comes to energy, there are two things to remember: it's extremely fickle while simultaneously being very precise. In order to wield energy in a powerful way, you cannot dabble in spiritual matter. It's not a hobby or a Saturday afternoon; it's a way of life. When you are true to your spiritual practice the external, trivial chattels of life do not influence you. They do not challenge your equilibrium because you are connected to your soul. You're grounded and can see past the illusions, especially the ones called Jane. Rather than living the horizontal ego path, your spiritual practice keeps you tapped in, tuned in, and turned on to the vertical path of higher consciousness. As I have gotten older, I have reached a state of equanimity that rarely falters. I certainly have days or weeks that are challenging, but unlike the past me, I have the ability to see past the illusion and see the deeper meaning through spiritual wisdom. I have an understanding now of what it is teaching me. Up to this point, I had oscillating spirituality. I read a ton of books, worked under several teachers, and did the so-called "work." But what I didn't realize was that my work was inside a small box of limiting beliefs, and when those beliefs were challenged, so was my ego. This kept me oscillating to only things that fit in to my ideologies and avoiding anything that challenged me.

The 3D human experience creates a very convincing reality that makes it seem real. It spikes our emotions, increases the heart rate, and we can see, feel, hear, and logically know the experience as if it's really happening to us. What I did not fully comprehend at this time was that each and every one of us creates our reality with our thoughts and emotions. From some dark corner of the recesses of my mind, I created Jane the real estate agent. I had read hundreds of books up to this point about this very concept, but it wasn't actualized until I experienced this moment in time. In other words, in order to expand your consciousness as a soul, you've had lifetimes of experiences to enrich the concept of yin and yang, to see and feel contrast in everything, and grow from it. You've explored things like forgiveness, love, hate, redemption, humility, pain, health, poverty, richness, lightness, and darkness. Each experience teaches you its contrast, or counter part, so you fully understand. For me, my small box of limiting beliefs prevented me from fully grasping the consciousness of what self-realization is: to really know myself and that I was the creator of all of it. Me. No one else. Even though the knowledge was there, it had not birthed into wisdom. And in order to absorb the knowledge, I had to be willing to see the forest for the trees, and I was too busy being lost in the desert.

Spiritual leaders like Delores Cannon, Wayne Dyer, Marianne Williamson, Gary Zhukov, Neale Donald Walsh, and many others shared this very wisdom, and lined my bookshelf. But until my consciousness was ready to fully unpack their words, fragments of misinterpreted information sat outside my box. Now when I return to these books from a place of higher perspective, I laugh out loud as the wisdom is hidden in plain sight. You, me, and everyone on this planet not only creates our own reality, but we also create it together. It all comes down to choice. Do you choose to play the victim and stay chained to limiting beliefs that you're not good enough, and life will always be against you? Or do you choose to take command of your life and turn things around? You are the creator and have more power then you've been led to believe. You are not your circumstances, but you are your thoughts and emotions. Break away from what you think it is and see all that your life can be. Only in that way can you regain your power and reach a state of equanimity.

Over the next five chapters, I am going to take you on a deeper dive into my system called the Top Five Disruptors™ to help you better understand my Feng Shui. But don't be fooled; this is not an analytical system. Here, we go beyond logical, and even philosophical thinking—which, let's be honest, has exhausted itself. Social existence has already taken us to grand intellectual heights. Now I am going to take you into the depths of the psychic womb where mythological memories can come alive again and help you reawaken the connection to your soul.

UNLOCKING YOUR POWER

Your limited understanding of all that is changes as you proceed up the vertical path of enlightenment. As you climb up the spiritual mountain, every step forward gains you another vantage point, and if you continue up, the more your view expands. With greater understanding, your wisdom deepens into compassionate acceptance, and you can start to see the divine plan. In the course of your journey, it's important that you continually get your house in order at each stage of growth to help you proceed forward, whether that's your personal house, meaning your personal Chi, or the Chi of your environment. It all matters. Only when you can see God in every aspect can you free yourself of limiting beliefs. Many of us have profound layers of programming and conditioning handed down to us that we take on as our own. Without realizing it, we have spent years molding and fixing a model from someone else's ideologies and never recognize that we can abandon it at any time. But you do have to be willing to revisit them again and again to embrace your own truth and find the many discriminations you've acquired along the way. Until you can supersede the limiting belief with open curiosity and acceptance, you stay stuck. If you continue to do the work, you continue to climb the mountain and gain new perspectives along the way. Take time to reflect on the beliefs you hold. Can you recognize which are your own, and which have been graciously handed down? Many are so intertwined into our very fiber, it can take years of unfoldment to recognize it. To rebuild a creed that is yours and yours alone requires great power. Your power. Unfortunately, many individuals have found it hard to open themselves up to such vulnerability. Through no fault of our own, our beliefs have created false expectations of what we might see, or rather what we want to see, and this limits our insight.

In Feng Shui, taking a commanding position is commonly associated with the position of your bed, desk, and stove. The focus is typically on physicality rather than spirituality. To me, it's so much more and requires both. It's about consciously connecting to who you are from a place of knowing. One cannot work without the other. Here, you stand empowered ready to explore your potency in both a physical and nonphysical way. In this way, as you connect with your personal power, the entire collective begins to rise.

Then, and only then, can you be and feel prepared to walk through the door of possibility. Without this sense of deep personal power you will not be inclined to feel like a powerful being. And this loss of personal power will reflect back to you in your environment. For example, a bed out of command is someone who is unable to see things, or someone, for what or who they are. The consummate victim riding waves of mood swings, insomnia and health issues. Life happening to them instead of for them. Or a desk against the window with the door to your back allows people to take advantage of you and walk all over you, keeping your perspective blocked.

There is much fulfillment in discovering your power, but it is a delicate path. In our society power is often associated with a mental model of patriarchy. Men are naturally able to tap into this energy stream and, in some instances, it can border out of control. However, in many cases, those extremities can be a smoke screen for insecurity. Power is not about controlling others; it's about taking command in all areas of your life, energetically speaking and physically to embody the best version of you. It's about tapping into a well of enthusiasm, committing with confidence and continuing up the climb to your uniqueness. Only when we allow ourselves to be acutely attuned to our bodies and our environment can we show up as our most authentic selves. It's seeing value in who you are, your strengths, your gifts, and even embracing your seeming faults, that you can move past the judgment and victimhood and have the ability to literally turn things around. Psychologically or physiologically, conscious or unconscious, it's your job to change the narrative, uproot those outdated beliefs, and apply new tools to unearth a new way of being. But to do this requires quiet, confident power.

TAKING COMMAND OF YOUR LIFE

Each of us has an opportunity to take the seeming chaos of our lives, the enormous ups and downs, and turn all of it into a profitable return of more joy, love and happiness. Taking command means you can assess from a higher perspective and see it for what it is: a chance to know its opposite. The greatest gift this Universe gives us is the free will to choose our unfoldment by way of contrast, as so eloquently said by Elisabeth Kubler-Ross:

> *"All the trials and tribulations, the greatest losses, things that make you say, "if I had known about this I would have never made it through," are gifts to you. It's like somebody has to temper the iron. It is an opportunity that you are given to grow. This is the sole purpose of existence on this planet Earth. You will not grow if you sit in a beautiful flower green and somebody brings you gorgeous food on a silver platter. But you will grow if you are sick, if you are in pain, if you experience losses, and if you do not put your head in the sand but take the pain and learn to accept it not as a curse, or a punishment, but as a gift to you with a very, very specific purpose."*
> On Life After Death, 1991, page 22, Elisabeth Kubler-Ross

It is through contrast that you learn to fight the fight. You can fall to circumstance and give up by playing the victim, or you can rise above it. Eventually, everyone has a point in their life where they lose their power. And everyone has points where they feel powerless. From this experience, you are forced to take a long, deep look at yourself and unwrap the gift that it is. It may take you years to recognize the omniscient being glowing within you, or it may take days, but each of you can take the conflict and turn it around. Your greatest tool and your greatest weapon is energy. Through contrast, you are forced to change your vibration. To shed the formalized energy of what was and turn it into what it can become, that is the authentic you. The highest version of you. If you fail to do this, you grind on old habits and habitual behavior and continue to lose your power.

We all want to know what our purpose is and why we are here.

Knowing is what changes your perception of life and gives you strength through all of life challenges. But so many are confused and stuck in the perpetual loop of smallness and familiarity, climbing only a few short steps up the mountain and then giving up. Such a directionless life results in consequences. Lack of knowledge depletes your power, and you can become destructive. This results in failed relationships, an unfulfilling career, a strained family dynamic, and constantly feeling powerless. Without a clear sense of self-understanding, you cannot comprehend the bigger picture. So when things appear to go wrong, it can be difficult to respond appropriately. But if you learn to work with your energy in a positive way, you become the best expression of your personal power.

When I share this story about this time in my life with students, they often ask if I practiced Feng Shui. The answer is yes and no. I haphazardly had been doing Feng Shui, but I wasn't taking the time to develop relationships with these homes, and I'm not sure you could call what I was doing solid energy work. With such an immense loss of personal power, I was essentially a car with no gasoline.

In earlier chapters, I discussed how important it is to do energy work with a fine-tuned instrument. It's never perfect, but neither is life, so you do the best you can. But if you're stressed out, overwhelmed, or anxious, that means your energy system is taxed, and you're not doing solid energy work. Your system is incoherent, and that's exactly why my Feng Shui during this time frame wasn't working. How could it? I was completely fried, and my energy was a tornado. However, as you read these words, it's important to know that this is the wheel of life. You're going to have ups and downs. You are also going to have times in your life that overwhelm you. But you do have a choice. You can always change directions, and it's never too late to take command of your life. We are all human. Each and every one of us makes mistakes, and spiritual work is a vertical path that's rarely a straight line. It's going to be hard and messy to climb, but it is possible, so pack a bag and bring snacks!

The most challenging thing for me during this time was rereading spiritual texts from spiritual masters and feeling like a damn failure! I was searching for my power and had moments of hopelessness. Would I ever be able to find it again? Despite that, I was inspired by these books because what they said rang true deep in my soul. So, inch by inch, I started to dig myself out of despair, believe in my ability to heal, and get back on track with what I was meant to do. I mention this because this is a common side effect for many humans going through a difficult time. Our ego can get in the way of meaningful spiritual work, and your old belief systems can come crashing in to remind you that you're not good enough, worthy enough, smart enough, or talented enough, and that's what got you in this mess in the first place. Comparison is the thief of joy, so remind yourself that everyone, including the teachers you admire, were once new to their spiritual practice too.

Many of the spiritual books available teach about self-realization and intention as being the keys to the vertical path of higher consciousness to get you *there*. Using tools like meditation help you get "there" and tap into your truth, which leads to your unquestionable power. But where exactly is *there*? What does *there* mean? And how do you know that you want to go *there*? Let it be said, my intention with this book is not to preach you into spiritual awareness by way of Feng Shui. My intention is to give you tools to overcome the battle within yourself so you can realize there are options. I'm going to show you the door where there once was a wall, and it's up to you to walk through it. And of course, my wish is that you continue up the mountain, and together we shall all rise.

WHAT IS COMMANDING POSITION

One of the most important things I learned from this time in my life is that we grow from experiences, not lessons as many of us have been told, and we have the choice to choose a better path, to create and manifest a different reality. This is how you tap into your power. One of the most universal teachings across all schools of Feng Shui is the concept of taking command or command position. This principle is not only a vehicle for commanding power from your environments but also fuses into all areas of your life. In my opinion, you cannot have one without the other. For example, if your personal Chi is experiencing a loss of power, it's unlikely your environment will feel uncomfortable if you're out of command. If your Chi is strong, a commanding position is undoubtedly the only way your environment won't feel off. Otherwise, you feel restless until the energy is in alignment and fixed.

What exactly is command position? It's simple. Always situate yourself in the best, most powerful position in any situation to stay safe and in charge. This improves health—mentally and physically—improves clarity, and helps you tune into spiritual wisdom without being distracted by fight or flight responses. The easiest way to do this in your environment is to ensure that no matter where you sit, stand, or lie down, you can always see the door. It's basic built-in evolution that protects you from getting eaten by the saber-toothed tiger. In its simplest explanation, it's a way to feel safe, secure, and empowered.

As we have learned, everything affects your energy, and this is why cultivating your Chi daily is so important, no matter your level of spiritual expertise. Even though you may have been doing a spiritual practice for years, or maybe you just started, cultivation takes time, attention, and patience. Without it, you'll find it difficult to take control of anything in your life, like I did. I was not situating myself in the best position or setting myself up for any kind of success, because I had lost my power. At that time, I was telling myself I was a conscious individual because I had been "doing the work" for thirteen years, albeit oscillating. Dipping your toe in the pond versus swimming in the great ocean are two very different things. You must always remember that you are the outcome of the equation. So if you want to maximize your situation, you have to choose to take action to improve it. Be open to change and have the humility to receive the shifts necessary to take command of your life.

As mentioned earlier, three of the most important areas in your home where commanding position is always considered is the bed, desk, and stove. This also applies to your office outside of the home. Command position benefits fortune, increases success and luck, and it improves health. The biggest side effect that I have seen due to clients being out of command is lack of luck and good health. Because without command, you lack personal power. And if you have an environment where you are out of command, and you are not cultivating your Chi, it could result in a lot of stress and chaos. Feng Shui involves many moving parts in order to ensure auspicious positioning of your energy. It requires a symbiotic relationship between your Chi and the Chi of your environment to create a cohesive marriage of order. This is the vertical path of Feng Shui cultivation. By doing the work, you set clear intentions about the direction you seek, hiking further up the mountain. But one cannot occur with out the other. When it comes to energy, you have to maximize yourself and your surroundings to keep yin and yang balanced. Only in this way can Chi flow and results can happen. Otherwise, you create a scrambled mess of energy and attract Jane into your life.

BED POSITION

Placing your bed in an ideal location in any bedroom, but most importantly the bedroom you sleep in, empowers you to achieve the best position for better sleep, better health, and smoother energy. While this is important for everyone reading this, it cannot be stressed enough: if you are going through a challenging time in your life, it is extremely important that you place your bed in a commanding position to keep your personal Chi and the Chi around you as smooth as possible.

I often get clients who tell me that their best position is East or some other specific direction. I do not practice directional Feng Shui because I have learned that it can put you in harm's way. Perhaps you've been told that your best direction is Southwest, but if this location puts you out of command, with the door behind you, you can create a lot of unnecessary issues in your life. The concept of the commanding position is that the position of the bedroom door is far more important than the direction the bed faces in order to feel calm and safe. And the further it is from the door, the more control you feel over your life. The principle may sound far out, but it's basic evolution. The wider the scope of vision you have from your bed, the safer you feel. If you cannot see the door you can't see when someone approaches or enters your door. This can leave you feeling uncertain and on edge. It can also greatly affect your mood. Not being able to see the door creates subconscious stress, which over time creates unrest in the nervous system. Suddenly you start feeling out of control and overwhelmed, and you don't know why!

You may argue, well I've had my bed on the door wall for twenty years and I'm just fine, Amanda. Well, I beg to differ. How do you know for sure? Are you experiencing health issues? Nervous disorders? Insomnia? How about any heart issues, which is very common with folks who are not in command. I always tell my clients, unless you know for sure, move the bed and see what happens.

In the fall of 2012, after only a year, I had been booted from Sheffield College of Design and Feng Shui for lack of funds, so I decided to take matters into my own hands and dive back into some of my old Feng Shui books and DIY my way out of this mess. One of them followed the compass philosophy and, according to my calculations, my best position was Northwest. The only way I could achieve this position in the home of that moment was to put my bed on an angle. I wasn't really keen on any of this but my Chi was very spastic and uncultivated, so throwing spaghetti at the wall to see what would stick seemed totally reasonable.

I tried this position for a month. I became very restless and couldn't sleep. My stress was getting worse, and I developed an ulcer. My insomnia continued to get worse, and I could not shut my brain off. I would dwell on the most trivial, stupid things all night and then wake up exhausted. I was irritable and cranky because of the lack of sleep, so finally I moved my bed back to the main wall where I was back in command. I still had stress. However, I was able to shut my brain off and sleep through the night. My insomnia went away, and I can't explain it, but I felt better. After that experience, I realized that my original teachings were right. Direction is the least important thing when it comes to being in command. Let it be said, I have respect for all schools and all methods and find that each has power-ful, meaningful wisdom, but when it comes to the commanding posi-tion, your bed should always be able to see the door. It is the only way you can regain alignment and plug into your power.

If moving the bed is not an option, the next best thing is to place a large mirror in your space that picks up the reflection of the door. It can be hung on the wall or use a beautiful floor mirror. This simple tool will bring your Chi to rest and allow you to feel safe.

A COMMANDING DESK

Without realizing it, many of us innately put our lives in a commanding position. Even though our modern world has dulled our instincts, we still have a few in place that we do subconsciously without realizing it. In ancient times, we would place ourselves in a cave with our backs to the back wall so that we could always be on guard to leap at an intruder. Instinctually, our one-entrance cave was synonymous with safety. Unfortunately, despite knowing this evolu-tion, we are sometimes swayed by other factors and deviate from the energetic path of positive Chi flow due to room layout, window placement, trying to save space, or the sheer fact that we want to look out the window. Let's face it, the idea of a tiger leaping at you, while problematic in the past, is most likely not going to kill you in the suburbs. With that said, more than any other Feng Shui principle, the desk placement is where I often get the most push back from clients. I mean, it's unlikely I'm going to get attacked at my desk, so can I just look at the birds?

I will leave you with this: A few years after my personal apoca-lypse, or as I like to call them, The Dark Ages of Amanda, I met Tom. He was looking to get more positive energy into his life, mainly to help his real estate business grow. He said that he felt stuck and that it was hard to get any real forward motion. He would take a few steps forward, get really excited, and then something unexpected would happen and he'd fall ten steps back—words describing a loss of feeling empowered. *Hey man, I hear ya Tom! If you only knew what I just went through! Not only did a tiger get into my cave, but the cave flooded, washed everything out and then the whole damn mountain fell down.* Okay, not really, but I knew where Tom was coming from. I set up a time to meet with Tom at his office. It was a lovely space full of books and clutter and a well-lived life. He immediately told me that he assumed it was the books and clutter messing up his energy flow. And while that can clog some things, I was drawn to the massive six foot desk shoved up against the wall.

"Tell me about your desk, Tom. Why do you have it up against the wall?"

He looked at me with a funny smirk and said, "Oh, I just love watching the squirrels. They jump from tree to tree and they chase each other, and they are just a delight to watch."

The problem with this scenario is that Tom is not only distracted from doing his job because he's being entertained by the squirrels, but he was also out of command. When your desk is out of command, meaning the door is at your back, you're literally missing out on everything. You can't see new opportunities or what's coming at you. And literally, things are going on behind your back. This scenario can cause business deals to fall through, clients to be dishonest, and you can have health issues from the anxiety of it all. Not to mention, in many cases I've seen many folks say they were "stabbed in the back." No way to feel empowered in that scenario!

When I mentioned the desk to Tom, he didn't seem convinced. I don't think he wanted to give up his squirrels. So, I asked Tom to give me thirty days. Let's swing your desk around for thirty days and see what happens. We didn't do anything else other than swing the desk around. Within a week of us moving his desk, three deals came through that he had been sitting on for over a year. One had been dragging on and had run into one snag after another, but Tom "suddenly" had the realization that there was a loophole to get around the issue. By moving his desk, we literally turned things around, and after that he was convinced that he no longer needed to watch his squirrels. Without even realizing it, Tom got his power back!

TAKING COMMAND OF YOUR STOVE

Everything is energy. In Feng Shui, health and wealth are intimately related, mainly because good health is the foundation for building wealth, and wealth is the foundation for buying better food. And, you could argue, wealth helps you buy better ways to care for yourself. Your stove is a key player in the story of your wealth and health. It's the springboard for creating the best quality Chi in yourself and your environment. Its condition, placement, and overall aesthetic are contributing factors to the health of you and everyone in your family. Treat either in a poor fashion and both will suffer the consequences.

Unlike any other area in your environment, the stove is the leading energy generator for better health and finances. It provides nourishment and vitality to all areas of your life but chief among them is personal power. Why? Because your family's financial welfare and health are energetically tied to it. Get these factors right and you'll experience family harmony, freedom from legal issues, better finances, and it improves how you feel. Get this area wrong and you'll see overall well-being decline, disharmony, and a loss of finances. One enhances power, the other depletes it. The good news is, regardless of your current status, you can always improve your situation simply by adjusting and cleaning your stove.

Your body is a temple. Albeit temporary, but it's where you inhabit this incarnation to do the work of remembering who you are and becoming enlightened. Assuming you continue up the mountain and expand your awareness, each step becomes a breadcrumb that reminds you of your almighty self. As you read this book, you're going to come to the understanding that the care of your your environment reveals your level of awareness and vice versa. Equally coexisting, you and your environment work together to continue up the mountain on your journey. The more your environment reflects your Chi, the more you can embody health and well-being. The more you reflect your environment, the more it can embody health. Not only is the saying true, "We are what we eat," but it's a reminder of how the food we eat affects the Chi of our body and our home. In many ways, the stove is where we have the opportunity to increase valuable vibrations in many areas of our life. As mentioned in Chapter 6, this is about conscious eating and deliberate cooking. There is no better place to attend to how you prep, chop, and cook than to radically change your thoughts around the stove. It is the epicenter of the kitchen, and it determines if the energy is aligned or needs work. From chopping, preparing, and cooking a meal, this can be characterized as energy transformation in motion. You drive your Chi into the entire process, then you consume the Chi and manifest it into another form of vibration. This is why eating clean, organic foods is so important to ensure the best possible energy consumption.

In addition to eating well, always be concerned with the vibrations associated with the source of your foods. For example, there is a vast difference between food grown by Monsanto and the local boutique, organic farmer down the road.

Years ago, I had a friend tell me that she was getting really sick after eating fruit from her local grocery store. After doing research, she discovered that this particular farm was allowing inmates from the local prison to collect their fruit to reduce labor costs. My friend was extremely sensitive to energy, and she was picking up on the low vibrational energy coming in contact with this fruit. So not only must you consider the source of your food, but you also need to be mindful of the energy it brings to your stove. All energy matters. As mentioned in the previous chapter, there is a Sufi saying, "If a person eats with anger, the food turns to poison." I'd take this a step further. If you cook with anger, the food turns to poison.

GETTING GOOD VIBRATIONS

One of the highest ways to empower the cook and increase the vibration of the energy surrounding your food is to place a mirror behind your stove, if it's up against a wall, and your back is to the door. This ensures that the cook's energy is protected while they stand at the stove and can safely prepare a meal. If a cook is startled due to a stove's placement, consciously or subconsciously, that energy vibration travels into the food. Not to mention, it can be detrimental to the cook's health and wealth over time.

In 2004, Masaru Emoto, a Japanese businessman and author, proved that human consciousness could affect the molecular structure of water. His book, *The Hidden Messages in Water*, showed examples of water molecules being affected by speech. In addition, his work demonstrated that water is shaped by the environment, thoughts, and emotions. Fascinated by this concept, I did an experiment on rice. You can see the results on YouTube. The video is called *Can Words Spread Love*. For two weeks I yelled angry words and sent angry thoughts to one container, and sent loving thoughts and words to another container. To my amazement, the container with angry words started to grow mold within a few short days, and the other container was completely clean even after two weeks.

The words and emotions you have matter, especially around the food you consume. By creating a sense of safety and protection for your cook, the energy feels calmer and translates to better health and wealth. It is important that you use a solid mirror that is kept clean and isn't antique glass, broken, or distorted. Mirrors reflect who we are and also represent the mind. So never have a mirror with chips, cracks, etchings, or glazing. It's also important to keep your stove clean and to use each burner equally. This is, after all, a wealth generating appliance that also generates good health if used appropriately. So use all burners to ensure that your stove is providing you a healthy and generous return.

If it's not possible to hang a mirror on the wall behind your stove, you can also place a free standing mirror off to the side. Make-up mirrors or convex mirrors found at auto part stores work really well. Another way to increase your personal power, wealth, and health is to get your stove tuned up regularly. Any portion of the stove that does not work creates an impediment to your well-being and income.

Mirrors are great tools to double the burners and smooth the Chi around the stove. But if that won't work, another great way to protect the cook and stabilize the energy in your kitchen is to hang a chime or faceted round crystal from the ceiling directly above where the cook stands. This helps keep unwanted energy out of the kitchen and increases positive energy.

And finally, it goes without saying, keep your stove spotless. The cleanliness of the stove is a direct reflection of how you feel and the money you attract. Keeping the stove clean on a regular basis ensures fresh wealth opportunities in your life. Food, health, and wealth are intimately tied together. Dirt, grime, and food scraps create stagnant energy, making it harder to attract better health and stronger wealth. A dirty stove can also contribute to financial entanglements and other money problems. The strongest manifestation of Chi, or life force, is putting a disciplined practice in place to maintain the health of your food and stove. Otherwise you might attract scoundrels.

THE SPIRITUAL SIDE OF TAKING COMMAND

Sooner or later there comes a point in your life when you wake up and start questioning reality. Some will say it doesn't exist; others will say it's all an illusion; and others still will call you plain nuts for asking the bigger questions. Moment by moment, it all seems like a random framework of meaninglessness until an interesting thought crosses your mind and makes you question, "But what if there's more?" As a species we cannot help but be attracted to a world view that could be more harmonious, divinely ordered, and peaceful. As Plato promised, "Things are taken care of far better than you could possibly believe." Yet superficially, reality seems confusing and chaotic, where the ungodly Janes of the world can flourish and steal your power unknowingly. In the *Republic*, Plato describes the ascent of the mind in four stages. Beginning in ignorance, we don't even realize that there's anything worth knowing. This is certainly the bottom of the mountain. Then we move into the stage of Opinion, a knowledge of sorts based on almost nothing. We take a few steps up the mountain and decide this is all there is. By education and study, we can move to Reason. Perhaps this broken, narrow, and scary path can lead us somewhere? But only through honing and sharpening of our skillsets can we finally move into Intelligence. This is the ascent that makes me come to the conclusion that the more I climb up the mountain, the better I can see. Alas, with spiritual wisdom does come personal power!

You can prepare for it, and plan for it, but there is no guarantee that you'll find success in it. Because preparing and planning are based in ego, and commanding your power is learning how to tap into the supernatural. At each level, you can only achieve a higher spiritual status by unfoldment of *it*, but what exactly is *it*? Can *it* be logically explained? Do we actually understand *it*? Or are we trying to think our way through *it* when instead it's more of a feeling? This is where the constructs of the mind can tear apart the influence of mystical enthusiasm and make magic seem mundane. Can your environment help you take command of your life? Help you set boundaries? Stand in your truth? See beyond the veil of illusion? Yes. In fact, if you listen to *its* whispers, it reveals to you that you don't have to endure trauma and tragedy to glean spiritual transformation.

In truth, you don't have to think about *it* at all. The universe gives you countless opportunities to discover your power dependent only on your willingness to acknowledge the subtle clues along the way, so you can lean into your divine potential. But this can only occur if you shed those limiting beliefs you've stayed so lovingly tethered to, so you can increase your vibration, AKA power.

As soon as you enter the world of the sacred, symbolic, and philosophical, your heart opens up to new influences that stimulate you in unimaginable ways. You begin to feel as never before, the wonderfully intricate beauty of Creation. The *it* factor. You see the artistry that's far above human intelligence or reason. Each of us is capable of comprehending far more than we might realize, but with wobbly training wheels that don't even belong to us, we have held ourselves back for lack of belief in ourselves, scared we'll crash and burn, or worse, disappoint someone!

All knowledge of the Universe is deep within you. It is through experience that you learn to flesh it out. As big events happen, your energy is expanded and you are forced to make a decision, you are forced to grow, you are forced into your almighty power. Think about times when you are in equanimity. There's no fight; there's no surge. But when a big life event occurs, you're suddenly placed at a cross-roads and forced to choose. Will you allow Jane to win, or will you find the power to see beyond it? Through cultivation, you can access that power and see past the illusion. You can see it for what it is. But if you oscillate to only things that fit into your model of beliefs you'll restrict yourself from seeing and experiencing all that is and be forever stuck in a loop of sameness.

This cosmic creative process gives you physical and spiritual tools to navigate up the mountain, whether it's Jane, Feng Shui, or some-thing else. We all have the ability to create a new reality simply through the power of our vibration. And we have the power to over-come all circumstances that appear to be real. By learning to tap into your power and adjusting your power positions within your environ-ment, you can discover the inherent balance and harmony that exists in all situations and create something new, like how to take command of your life by cultivating your Chi and paying attention to your bed, desk, and stove.

EXERCISE

SUNSHINE BUDDHA

The Sunshine Buddha exercise helps to purify the body, mind, and spirit. It is used to stimulate and heal your Chi and restore its balance. It can also help release you from the pressures or stress of society, your family, and your environment.

Method:

1.With your hands above your head, stand in the sunshine with palms up and feet shoulder-width apart. Turn your head up to face the sun. If you are too weak, you may do this portion sitting down.

2. Visualize the sunlight entering through the center of each palm, swirling down, getting warm, and entering in through the third eye. (An area between the brows.) Visualize light traveling down through your body very quickly and exiting through the bottom of your feet. Allow the arms to rest.

*You can also visualize that any bad action created by your body is moving out of your feet with the light.

3. Raise your arms back up and visualize the sunlight entering each palm and the middle of your forehead. It rushes down very quickly and out the feet. Quickly, the light boomerangs back to your

head, exiting through your two palms and the forehead. Visualize it cleansing the body.

4. With arms back up, visualize sunlight reentering your body through the three points and rushing back out the feet. Now visualize it circling back up moving slowly upward in a spiraling, circling motion around your vital organs, joints, or any problem areas.The movement is counter-clockwise. The sunlight cleanses every cell and pushes all bad Chi up and out of your body. Releasing all illness and bad fortune.

5. Lower the arms and repeat this exercise nine times for nine or twenty seven days. This exercise can be done all at once, or the nine cycles each day can be broken up throughout the course of the day. For example, one cycle done in the morning, and seven more throughout the day and the final one repeated just before bed. Or you can do all nine cycles first thing in the morning. Use the sunlight from this exercise to boost your Chi, to heal any ailments, break away from karma, and heal illness.

8

SHUT THE FRONT DOOR!

"The most beautiful experience we can have can be found in the mysterious."
Albert Einstein

*A*s I stared at the stack of floor plans on my desk, I contemplated the day ahead of me and wondered what I should start working on first. I had two guests lined up for the podcast that day, writing that needed to be done, and I planned on squeezing in a yoga class at noon. I started to write down what I wanted to get accomplished and then clearly got nudged to look at the floor plans. Typically when this occurs, and you know that *feeling* that won't go away, I've learned it's better to listen or the voice will get louder.

I picked up the stack of floor plans and one house in particular jumped out. Ah yes, this is the one screaming at me. Simply put, when I review plans, the homes speak to me. It's no different than how BoBo had spoken to me so many years ago. Only now, I have numerous homes vying for my attention and, just like humans, some are gracious, others have a quieter demeanor, and some are gregarious and loud. This house was an extrovert. She had things to say, and I needed to pay attention. What's important to mention is that all homes have details within them that are text book Feng Shui, however, it is the deeper inspiration, the language of home, where the rubber meets the road. Over the years I've simply learned to listen and trust, and you'll need to do the same. Honor your inspirations. The more you do, the louder they'll get! Now, if I don't listen, they intrude on my meditation practice, show up in yoga class, or pop in while I am out loving on nature. I once had a house blast into my yoga class while I was in downward dog. The owners were about to cut down her favorite tree. As I continued to stretch into my downward dog, the house said excitedly, "Should you be here? We need to do something about my tree!"

In Chapter 5, you learned all about the power of energy. When it comes to wielding energy, your greatest weapon is *you*. Trusting in your own ability and knowing that there are greater truths beyond your five senses comes to you only when you cultivate and care for your Chi. Now you may be saying to yourself, *I don't talk to houses, Amanda. You do that.* But here's the real truth: When you learn to go past your intellect and *feel* your way into understanding what she needs, that's when the spiritual Feng Shui journey begins. It will look different for everyone. But as you add more spiritual matter into your life and follow the principles in this book, your life will open up in odd, mysterious, and magical ways. You'll start by experiencing what you think is a coincidence, maybe you'll hear something new that piques your interest in a different way, or perhaps you'll be inspired to do something "out of the blue." Don't be fooled. This is intuition, and if it refers to your environment, often the messages are coming from your home. Trust me when I say, each and every one of you has this ability. Problem is, like me, most of you want to skip to the hocus-pocus. You want to skip over grade school and high school and jump straight into what you think is college-level Feng Shui. Unfortunately, your home's energy is subtle and fleeting, and only a fine-tuned instrument will be capable of becoming a vibrational match to her communication. So grade school it is, my friend.

Learn to trust and develop a relationship with your home. At this point, she should have a name, so refer to her often, talk to her spirit lovingly, and she will guide you. We all have this ability, no matter what you've been told or what you've learned in the past. In fact, feeling Chi is the easiest, fastest way to learning how to speak the language of home, or any energy for that matter. Start by driving down a street that has low Chi. Don't know what I'm talking about? Trust me when I say, you'll recognize it immediately. The yards aren't cared for, the homes have chipped paint and broken windows, or maybe a roof that needs repaired. The home-owners here are likely sad and beaten down. Now drive down a street where the yards are pristine, the homes are cared for, and the neighbors are happy. Can you sense the difference? Can you see it? Can you feel it? That my friends, is Chi. Even if you're new to speaking its language, you can *feel* it. That is the spirit of a healthy home. Honor how you feel, because those emotions are information communicating with you. If you find yourself thinking, "This area is really run down," or "Man, no one takes care of their homes here," or other notions that bring notice to how things look, that is lack of Chi. It's dull, dead, and lifeless. This has nothing to do with money. This has to do with a homeowner's pride and desire to want to care for their home, and if they don't have it, that lack of motivation is them being affected by the lack of Chi in the area. Remember, Below the Cross Energy is heavy and dense. It's like moving through quicksand.

GOING BEYOND TEXTBOOK FENG SHUI

The beginning of the phenomenal world begins at the entrance to your home. It acts as a portal, taking you beyond time and physical surroundings, and catapults you into a reality of yin yang opposites that constantly provokes you to bring it into harmony. As your home mirrors your energy and reflects back to you changing states of Chi, you will learn that experience becomes more relative through emotion. When you learn to break away from logic, tap in, tune in, and turn on the light within you, you can adapt to the harmony of the universal intelligence.

As I reviewed the house plan that was shouting at me, I heard very clearly, "digestive issues." However, I didn't see anything within the plan that suggested this, so I continued to look.

"Ok my love," I said out loud, "I see possible financial issues, loss of resources, maybe loss of love."

And then inspiration burst in again more loudly, "Yes, yes, and digestive issues!"

So I wrote it down and circled it. This is where the *listening* and the *trust* comes in. Take note of your first impressions before logic and reasoning gets in the way. I'm the queen of letting logic crash the party in its usual dramatic fashion. So learn to recognize it and go with your gut, no matter how convincing that logical stance seems.

Now that this house had my attention, I looked more closely. One thing that really stood out to me was the front entrance. Something was going on here, but what was it? Thinking felt off. It was blocked somehow, and the best I can describe it, it felt inflamed. Something was irritated. But as I reviewed the plan further, I wasn't sure. I couldn't put my finger on what *it* was. Maybe I was having an off day and the information I felt was incorrect? As a side note, everyone on my team always laughs out loud when I exclaim to have an "off day." I'll hand off the plan stating, "I'm not really sure, I think this is what they might be experiencing but I may be wrong." That would be my logic crashing the party. Luckily, this house was determined. She kept guiding me back to the front door and letting me know that her homeowner was experiencing some sort of digestive issue.

This home didn't tell me her name, but she was sad, and then I realized it was because she hadn't had a voice. No one was listening to her. (Err, and here I was doing the same about digestive issues!) She was exasperated and irritated. I could *feel* that no one was listening and it discouraged her. And despite questioning the information myself, because I couldn't make sense of it, she had my attention. I highlighted the digestive issues and then listed the other things I saw in the plan. I handed the plan off to my project manager, Deborah, and then went on with my day. I figured the gal or guy who owned the house would resonate with some of my crazy musings and that would be enough to grab their attention too.

Many esoteric things like Feng Shui are not understood. My system is simple. If you are interested in working with me, you contact my team, you send in your floor plan, and I give you my feedback. I'll typically spit out three to five facts that are undeniably showing up in your floor plan. If it resonates, you decide if you want to move forward with your healing. Because I'm typically a ten out of ten for results, you'd think I'd learn to trust myself, but I still have days where I question if I am hearing and feeling things correctly. What can I say? I'm human. So, when I tell you to listen and trust your own inspirations, just know, I'm not always taking my own advice. I understand the questioning and uncertainty. It's been over twenty years, and I'm still learning how to shut off my left brain and just go with it. But I will say, the more you do it, the easier it gets!

A few hours later, Deborah came strolling into my office, "As usual, you nailed it. But the nail in the head for her was the *digestive issues*. She was just diagnosed with Celiac Disease, and it's made her feel really foggy headed."

Shut the Front Door! I almost didn't include that in my notes. But once again the house never steers me wrong. Ever. Learn to trust and listen to your gut feelings. Trust and listen to your home. Always go with your first inspiration and honor it. Even if it's crazy, even if it ends up being off, the more you trust her whispers and gut feelings, the easier it will be to communicate with her.

The key here is the cultivation of your Chi. This goes way beyond textbook Feng Shui. When you learn to maintain a harmony between the inner self and your surroundings, equanimity can be fully achieved. This is the entrance into phenomenon that fashions your reality, and it's up to you, and your readiness to act on how you move forward without deviating.

YOUR EMOTIONS CARRY THE KEY TO EVERYTHING

What makes humans so unique is our ability to feel and express emotions. Our world is literally expressed, created, and cultivated via the emotional five senses. Even though we've been taught to suppress them most of our lives, emotions are Chi energy infused with a purpose. We have a choice to take them up or take them down. It's that simple. They play such a significant role in creating our experiences that we may forget what we had for dinner last night but we can remember in great detail where we were when the twin towers came down, or how we felt the day we got our first car, or the devastatingly clear memory we hold the day we lost a loved one. It is your emotions that connect you to your experiences, and they are the key to trusting other-worldly expressions of the unseen. Think about it. Most circumstances in your life are neutral, but it is your emotions (energy in motion) that make that experience either good or bad and memorable.

> *People will forget what you said, people will forget what you did, but people will never forget how you made them feel.*
> Maya Angelou

While mental prowess makes many people in today's society feel superior, it is your ability to translate emotions that will help you achieve more and go further in your life. It's the reason emotional intelligence is growing great momentum in many companies when it comes to hiring new employees. Emotions carry the key to everything. It is through them that you can read a person or an environment in an instant and tune in to the truth. In fact, your emotions interpret Chi faster and more accurately than any mental capacity can. It is through a system that surrounds you called the emotional body that stems from the electric field of the heart, which FYI, is your personal Chi. It is literally your personal Wi-Fi system that reads, interprets, and converses with everything around you and signals to you whether you are safe, have reason to be anxious, enveloped in love, or about to have a lot of fun! It's also what carries you, your thoughts, and emotions to every cell in your body, and it's constantly communicating with your world. Think about various feelings you've had during certain events. Better yet, think of common phrases we've all expressed like, "My heart leapt for joy," or "I had a sinking feeling in my gut." These emotions act as a Richter scale to better understand, interpret, and communicate the reality around you. Contrary to popular belief, your emotions are far more superior, accurate, and powerful than any mental capacity is. In fact, according to Heart Math, your heart's magnetic field is five thousand times larger than the brain, and its electrical field is sixty times more powerful than the brain, yet mental capacity has reined supreme for centuries. Your ability to communicate with others and your environment through your emotional intelligence is not only your direct line to God, it's a reminder that we are all one. It is the purest form of information devoid of thought clutter, preconceived notions, and learned behavior that keeps you in the status quo.

Understanding emotion is understanding Chi. When you can learn how to interpret your feelings, you can start speaking the language of the unseen, the Chi. Then and only then can you get acquainted with details that may be visually appealing but energetically devastating to your energy system. In Feng Shui, the most important thing to remember is Chi. Where is it coming from, how does it *feel*, and is it flowing properly? Only by understanding and learning how to interpret your emotions can you answer these questions and translate the Chi that surrounds you, because your emotions carry the key to everything. You are the most powerful Feng Shui instrument.

THE MOUTH OF CHI AKA THE FRONT DOOR

In our modern world, our environments affect us far greater today than our spaces of the past. Never has there been a time when ancient energy principles, like Feng Shui, are needed more than ever because never has there been a time when we spend more time indoors. Our environments influence our behavior, mood, and how we feel. They also influence the relationships we have with others. Combine that with skipping trips out in nature to fluff your Chi and instead choosing more time inside on electronics surfing your phone and you're bound to feel your Chi slump. Enter in anxiety, depression, fear, and worry.

Simply looking at the structure and style of the front door is not enough to determine its Chi. It's a great place to start, however, to determine if Chi energy is flowing or not, so you have to trust your first impression. How does it *feel*? In Feng Shui we call the front door the mouth of Chi. This one detail can reveal whether Chi is smooth and circulating throughout the home, or kinked and preventing forward movement in your life. Earlier when I was reading the floor plan that had digestive issues, I was giving you a glimpse at how I received a "first impression." It's important to know that they come in a whisper; they are light and fleeting and can be easy to miss. Logic will quickly step in to crash the party, and before you know it, the whisper has been replaced with a logical explanation of something else entirely different. This skill takes practice. We all harbor the ability, we just have to relearn what's been logically beaten out of us through years of social conditioning.

Because humans are spending so much more time indoors, interior design has become the main focus to achieve an appealing aesthetic to make us seemingly feel more comfortable. Problem is, a house may look beautiful and comfortable, have panoramic views, a killer zip code, or an ideal school district, but ignoring the Feng Shui can lead to unbalanced flow and strife in your life. One of the easiest ways to start wielding the energy around your home is to start experimenting with the front door. And just a side note, even though you may use the back door, side door or garage door as your daily door, the front door is still the front door. And in case you're wondering, one of the main drawbacks to ignoring your front door is it's importance in your overall snapshot to getting energy flow right. The thing to remember is what happens at the front door touches all areas of your life, so skip this important energy detail and you could haphazardly stack the cards against you! That's why the front door is an excellent place to start on your Feng Shui journey, especially if you're new to Feng Shui. There is no easier way to feel like a powerful energy ninja than manipulating energy at the front door and seeing results. Ka-pow!

In order to resolve issues that may be hindering you from moving forward in your life, look to your mouth of Chi. If you look to your own mouth as an example, what is it used for? Nourishment, right? So if your door doesn't work, can't work, or is prevented from working, then your home isn't getting proper nourishment it needs. It's essentially like having your mouth wired shut.

The front door represents many things. It not only nourishes all areas of your life but it's also symbolic of new opportunities, clarity of mind, and depending on its location according to the Bagua Map, could also represent your career, supportive people, or your ability to learn. It's also your voice to the world. So, as in the case of the gregarious floor plan I mentioned at the beginning of this chapter, her voice wasn't being listened to. Turns out the door was stuck, not working well, and this was affecting the homeowner's ability to think clearly and nourish herself. AKA, digestive issues!

Be sure to keep your door clean, free of cobwebs, and ensure that all the lights are working. Lights stir Chi! It's also important to make sure that the hardware is pretty and works well. Make sure the door isn't chipped, warped, or damaged. Everything in Feng Shui is a literal interpretation of energy flow. In other words, if your door is stuck, so is your health, luck, and opportunities.

WHAT HAPPENS IN VEGAS IS PURE GOLD!

Entrance doors should operate easily. If your door sticks, catches, or doesn't open or close correctly, think about how this affects your personal Chi, and how it could affect your environmental Chi over time. Let's say you go to open the door and it sticks just a little. The first time, it's no big deal and you may even forget about it, but fast forward six months from now and, as you approach the door, you're already subconsciously preparing for the stuck door that doesn't work well. UGH! Every time you approach the door, you deposit frustrated Chi. And let's not forget the door is also symbolic of many things like our thinking, luck, and new opportunities. Now those become frustrated, stagnant, and stuck too!

About a year ago, I flew up to Virginia to help a client get her Feng Shui right. As she put it, things weren't moving, finances were sticky, and no new opportunities were coming their way. Hmmm, sounds like the front door could use some love. Not only was the front door sticking, but the lock and door handle were not operating well. In fact, they often avoided using the front door, knowing that it would take effort. I encouraged the homeowner to hire a handy man to rehang the door, work on the hinges, and rework the hardware so it worked in an optimal manner. In addition, I asked that she polish up the hardware and oil it so it operated correctly, but also looked pretty.

These seemingly uneventful tasks may seem mundane, however, this is wielding energy in a powerful way. By cleaning up her front door, fixing the hardware, and getting a handyman out to make it operable, she changed her circumstances dramatically. Within three weeks of performing these tasks, she got the news that her husband, while on a work trip, had just won big in Vegas! Seems getting unstuck and shining up that hardware helped those new opportunities and good fortune roll in!

WIELDING ENERGY IN A COGNIZANT WAY

It's important to mention that whenever you do any kind of work on your home that you speak to her and let her know what's going on. In order to wield energy in an intelligent way, it's necessary to include her in your intentions, prayer, and devotions. I cannot tell you how many homes have come to me over the years, frightened about changes going on in their environment, especially if it involves a major remodel. Be cognizant of that energy and honor her. I learned this the hard way.

One day while in meditation, a house's energy came to me. I knew immediately who she belonged to. She was scared and frightened and didn't understand what was going on. There was a lot of chaos going on around her, including work trucks and work men. Her owners were new to her. The previous owners had owned this house for years and never took care of her. For years she laid in disrepair, with rotted trim, dry-rot doors, and unfinished projects. Not to mention gobs of trash and debris thrown about on her land. When the new owners took possession of her, their first order of business was to remodel the front door. They planned to rip out the single front door, move its location, and replace it with a beautiful double door. Having never been remodeled or loved on before, this disrupted the house energy, her spirit, and sent a ripple of Chi outward that, if not addressed, could have caused issues. Remember if your home's spirit is upset, she will act out via things breaking and going wrong. Everything is energy!

This home's energy was scared and simply needed to know what was going on. Whenever you are about to break ground on a property or remodel, always do a ceremony. In this situation, honor the old door for its years of service and perform a ceremony to invoke the new door for its future service. Calibrate and care for the energy, and most importantly, care for and honor your home's spirit. Chi must constantly change, move, and remain fluid in order to stay healthy. Your home is a mirror reflecting back to you changing states of Chi of other-worldly phenomenon. If you ignore these intrinsic workings, your health, relationships, and resources could be at stake. In our modern world, we have lost our connection to mystical breath. The purpose of this journey is not to explain or deny, but to facilitate a maturing of the heart so we can realize our union with God.

After I spoke to the home and asked her permission to perform the remodel, the homeowner and I did a beautiful ceremony to celebrate her new future with owners who love and adore her. Now her Chi is beaming and she's never looked or felt so good! Her energy is bright and her colors are no longer dulled. She *feels* dynamic and healthy. Months later, she came back to me in a meditation and her pride and love were palpable. She adored her owners and appreciated their concern for her welfare.

Be cognizant of how you treat the energy around you. Be mindful that your energy is commingling with the energy of your surroundings and vice versa. This is a symbiotic relationship, and when wielded in a respectful way, you create a sacred space called home.

ADDITIONAL THINGS TO TAKE INTO CONSIDERATION AT THE FRONT DOOR

Is Your Door Difficult to Find?

Not only does your environment communicate with you, but you are communicating with it, and what manifests is a direct reflection of your life experiences. If you are going through a traumatic time in your life like a divorce, grief, trauma, break up, death, chaos, or recovering through an embarrassing event, without realizing it, your Chi is likely screaming for an ascetic lifestyle. For example, you get the notion to move to the country or find a little gem that's cozy and quiet, but extremely hidden. Your home becomes a perfect expression of your psychological and spiritual state. And when you've been through a major life event that isn't positive, most people want to hide.

A few years ago, Luann reached out to me after her devastating divorce. As she put it, "After three years of living in my new home, I'm at my wits end and I need a floor plan reading. I am trying to rebuild my life after my divorce but no matter how hard I try to fix my home, I end up feeling frustrated. I find it difficult to move forward and get what I really want out of life. I keep getting passed up for promotions, no one listens to me, and no matter how hard I try, I can't find good help. I love my home, but I keep spending money on cosmetic changes, and it's not working and I'm throwing money out the door. Everything seems like such a struggle."

After reviewing her plan, I quickly realized why Luann was feeling so frustrated. Her house required over fifty steps up a tree-lined hill just to get her house! Once you finally arrived at the house, there were no clues as to where the front door was located. It required walking down the side of the house, entering a six foot tall gate and walking around the property to what appeared to be a door.

Luann's overall life experience was showing classic Feng Shui symptoms of a hidden front door. If your guest does not know how to find you, or where to go to find you, they literally deposit confused Chi. Which means you get confusing results. Over time, this will greatly affect the homeowner if they don't heal the energy.

One of the most difficult symptoms of a hidden front door is losing your voice in the community, especially when going through a difficult time. If your door is difficult to find, it can affect the entire household, challenge your career and affect luck in future events. Make the path to your front door obvious, and make it delightful. Fill it up with sculptures, signs, wind chimes, whirlygigs, or other moving objects, and anything else that literally shouts, "this way." Paint the front door an extraordinary color like red or any other color that acts as a siren that shouts to your guests, "You're at the right place!" Lighting a well-lit path is a great tool to guide your guests to the door, as well as spotlighting the actual door.

Is Your Door Blocked?

Upon entering your home, the first room you see has the most impact on your personal Chi and overall experiences. Since the front door can affect all areas of your life, it's imperative to get the energy right. Bottom line, it's either strengthening or weakening you; it's never neutral.

When it comes to your front entrance, it needs to be open and inviting. It shouldn't feel cramped or blocked or awkward in any way. If your door opens into a wall rather than a room, your life can become very difficult and you'll find yourself saying things like, "I feel so blocked."

Imagine this beautiful fluffy Chi swirling around you, and as you enter a home, your Chi slams into an adjacent wall that reverberates right back at you. This will without a doubt cause struggle and health issues. Not to mention, over time you'll deposit frustrated Chi every time you walk through the space because it will *feel* oppressive.

A few summers ago, I decided to get my real estate license to help people find more energetically valuable homes. I also wanted to help those who were trying to sell their homes fix energy kinks they didn't even know existed. One of my fellow brokers asked if I'd help do an open house on one of her listings. She had been hired by a builder who said the house had been on the market for a year. I found this very interesting, given the fact that it was a new construction home, so I knew something was up.

No surprise, when I arrived at the home, the entrance was not only cramped and awkward, but the door walked right into a wall. And this detail actually repeated in the owner's suite! No wonder this house wasn't selling!

This detail will affect everyone in the household, making life difficult and disappointing. Remember, this is the mouth of Chi, so if your mouth is hindered in some way, you can't get proper nutrition.

Do everything you can to open the space up. Change the door swing, hang a mirror up or put up a beautiful piece of art that captures you. Hang a beautiful crystal chandelier and add additional lighting. And don't forget to *feel* into the space. I see this detail a lot, and so many people experience frustration at their front door but quickly become apathetic about fixing it, consumed by their to-do lists.

Seeing Double

In Feng Shui, the entrance is called the mouth of Chi because it's the means by which Chi travels into your home and touches all areas of your life. If this is how your home gets nourishment, imagine if Chi couldn't flow properly. You may have a beautiful, spacious home, but if the entrance is congested, so is the Chi.

Double doors that are not equally used limit the flow of Chi, causing an array of issues. In order for Chi to be strong and healthy, the front door should be used often. This invites into your home the Chi of health, wealth, and happiness. But if you have a double front door, one door typically doesn't get used as often, if at all. This can leave you with a silent voice to the world, with lots to say but unable to speak up. Over time, one may withdraw giving less and less of themselves.

Ventilate the Chi often. Allow the old Chi to move out and the new revitalized Chi to come in and meander by operating both doors often. Make sure both doors work properly. As was the case of my client in Virginia, if the door isn't working well, luck of the entire household could be affected. Keep both doors operable, clean, and in good working condition. And keep the entry clean and tidy to keep your thinking sharp.

THE SPIRITUAL SIDE OF FRONT DOORS

In Greek mythology, doors are symbolic for transitions and beginnings. The Romans had a God of doors known as Janus, depicted with two faces, one looking to the past and the other to the future. All of the doors in your home are important, but none are as important as the front entrance. The front door acts as a portal, entering into a new energy, exiting an old. If that door is inoperable, or works poorly, it represents a dead end.

In Feng Shui the Front Door's symbolism is deep. Not unlike other unseen principles, its meaning is not to be taken lightly. Not only is it symbolic of your voice to the world, but it represents how you think, how you feel, and how your inner world is fed. Her energy can be fickle if not honored and cared for. On one hand, it provides great reward; on the other hand, non-believing is not without hazards. Careers can be lost or destroyed, health can deteriorate, and a community can vanish.

To a culture that is gratifying itself with skepticism, reasoning with Newtonian explanation to unseen forces, we are faced with a problem. Why? Humanity has put so much emphasis on what is physically perceivable through the five senses, and they consider that which is perceived to be all there is. Unfortunately, explanations are not always readily available. In fact, the physical world only comprises one percent of the whole cosmos, leaving the other ninety-nine percent of the subtle energies imperceptible to the human instrument. Can a front door truly be the link to new opportunities? The unseen has been a place we have forbidden ourselves to explore except in rare glimpses of unabashed imaginative thinking, which many of us stop exploring after the age of eight. Perhaps instead, we can enter into a twilight realm that seduces a new generation from the logical tasks of the day and entice them to explore the possibility of inner truths and *feel* a door's essence. The ancient mystics saw, felt, and experienced the front door as a magical portal, a portal that feeds our souls if given nourishment. Which do you want to experience? A new beginning or a dead end? The good news is, you have the choice to choose your fate.

EXERCISE

FRONT DOOR CHI

Flowers, window boxes, pottery, a garage? What do you see when you look at your home? What does her front entrance say to you? If you don't notice your front door, neither will your guests. Most home-owners never pay attention to the front of their homes, nor do they pay particular attention to the front door. They either brush past it, or they enter through another door. Before they know it, the cobwebs, broken lights, and dirt aren't even noticeable! One of the fastest and easiest ways to boost the Chi of your home is to care for her front door.

This is the mouth of your home. If it's not nurtured, neither is the energy entering your home that touches all areas of your life. So here's the takeaway: Take notice of your entrance. How does it look? Is it easy to find? Is it cluttered? Are you impressed? Do you feel uplifted when you see it?

Your entrance is where all new energy is welcomed into your home. If it's thriving, Chi quietly meanders into your home and flows throughout all areas of your life, supercharging it in really good ways. Strong vital Chi will boost your career, health, relationships, and even your finances! On the flip side, if an entrance is hard to find or messy, it's *hindering* the flow of good Chi and depleting all areas of your life. Think it doesn't matter? Think again. According to Feng Shui principles, Chi is life force energy. And guess what? Good or bad, it shows up in your home and reflects on all the things in your life. It can be open and inviting, or closed and restricted, hindering new opportunities. Which one do you want knocking?

So if your energy is feeling stuck or stagnant, or you feel like new opportunities are passing you by, it might be time to clean up and boost your front door!

15 EASY STEPS TO A BETTER FRONT DOOR

1. Keep your entrance neat and tidy and remove all clutter
2. Paint your door an exceptional color
3. Ensure that all lights are properly working
4. Remove anything that is cracked, broken or chipped
5. Decorate your door throughout the seasons to keep it fresh
6. Update old hardware with a shiny alternative
7. Avoid prickly plants like rose bushes around the door
8. Include a fresh welcome mat
9. Add good quality wind chimes
10. Prevent accidents by repairing pavers and cracked sidewalks
11. Include a bench or swing to portray a welcoming vibe
12. Wash the door regularly to remove dirt and grime
13. Remove all cobwebs
14. Make sure the doorbell is working
15. Keep the path to your doorway open and inviting

SHAPE SHIFTER

"First take the words, ponder their meaning, then the fixed rules will reveal themselves; but if you are not the right man, the meaning will not manifest itself to you."
Confucius

The mind rebels against the thought that unseen forces could be the result of experiences we have every day. But according to ancient knowledge, those unseen forces influence your reality whether you believe in it or not. This concept takes you out of subjection and places you into a position of responsibility. If receptive, this recognition teaches you to take a step back, have an open heart and open mind, and attribute your circumstances to something beyond intellectual comprehension. This is where the real work begins. When something starts to take shape, a seed that wakes up a supernatural lore deep within you and begins to appear in such a way that it's fairly clear what its final manifestation could be: inspiration. This is the power of your home's shape, and there is no better place to tap into such inspiration than that of the shape of your environment and her vernacular.

Within the shape of your home lies a world in which a language of your psyche is expressed. Suppressed by centuries of logical individuation, many have lost a connection to myths and symbols that are both illuminating and valid, yet looming in plain sight within your home's shape. It's time that you tune into this higher wisdom so that you can reboot the rhythm of the cosmos deep within you and access a psychic strata of undeniable mysticism that's ready to lift the veil of the human ego and plunge you into spiritual symbolism.

The shape of your environment reveals either harmony or discord in how Chi flows. Ideally, the shape of a home should be rectangular or square. Good architecture is like professional ballroom dancing, where smooth movement, beautiful stature and visual appeal embody rhythm, flow, and resonance. There is awe and delight and everything creates a pleasing, harmonious experience. You can *feel* it.

When shapes are balanced, so is the energy because there is divine order. This is evidenced through our numerical system and the divine golden ratio which can be found throughout history from the Mona Lisa to Notre Dame. Divine symmetry, better known as Sacred Geometry, is essentially God's fingerprint on our planet. The Golden Ratio of the Pythagorean Theorem, Phi, and the Fibonacci Sequence has a fascinating correlation and meaning that leads us to the bedrock where mysticism and intellect intersect. The beauty behind this is its appearance of balanced perfection found in life, art, music, architecture, spiritualism, and other-worldly wisdom. When this ratio is out of alignment, so is the energy and how things *feel*.

SACRED GEOMETRY

Sacred Geometry represents all of creation. On a subconscious level, it reminds us that everything is connected and it all comes from the same blueprint, hence, the Flower of Life. This geometric symbol is the basis for all other patterns in the Universe. It is a symbol of overlapping circles that can go on infinitely and constructs all other geometric forms within it, like Archangel Metatron's Cube that represents polarities of unified creation, and the divine supportive energy of the Merkaba, just to name a few. As you read this, these may be symbols you've never heard of. Unfortunately, many cultures have lost connection to myths and symbols because of logical systemization.

The idea of Sacred Geometry stems from the examination of patterns and their relationship to the natural world. At its seemingly basic origin, it's the study of drawing various circles and how they overlap. On the surface, it can sound elementary, but on deeper analysis it begins to reveal a highly intelligent system of lines and curves that construct the entire universal order.

It's within sacred geometry that we reach beyond the controllable and explainable 3D world and enter into a realm where desire for greater understanding guides us into undeniable heavenly imprints. Rather than unwittingly drifting with the current of the rational mind, we intuitively witness celestial notions that prove greater intelligence exists. This catapults us into a tug of war where each individual must arrive and adjust to the fated order that Heaven is indeed on Earth, if we choose to see it. Here, the framework of mysticism and reason can merge and be emphasized with great enthusiasm.

To work with Sacred Geometry and understand its presence is to open up to the womb of creation. It allows you to engage with the inherent harmony of the natural world and unite to a higher state of being. Traditionally, it was foundational that sacred buildings such as temples, mosques, megaliths, monuments, and churches utilize the concept of Sacred Geometry in their architecture. Not to mention, sacred spaces such as altars, sacred meeting groves, holy wells, religious art, and tabernacles would also employ divine proportions.

Ultimately, whether fully recognized or not, Sacred Geometry is a clandestine world view of pattern recognition, a complex system of symbols involving space, time, and form. These basic patterns of existence are recognized as sacred because they connect us to the Great

Mysteries and the Golden Ratio. By studying the architecture of these patterns and relationships, their connections to one another and us, insight is gained into the unseen mysteries, the laws and lore of the Universe.

THE GOLDEN RATIO

The Golden Ratio is a special number that adds up to 1.6180033…and theoretically goes on to infinity. This number has been discovered and rediscovered so many times that it has arrived at many different names like the Golden mean, the Golden section, divine proportion, Phi, etc. Historically, the number can be seen in art, music, sculpture, and architecture. Examples like the Great Pyramids, The Parthenon, and The Last Supper have been studied extensively to show its Golden Ratio. But even everyday items like snail shells, flower petals, and hurricanes showcase the Golden Ratio as a fundamental constant of nature. How cool is that?

The Golden Ratio is considered the most universally binding of mathematical relationships, which might explain why our brains seem hard-wired to respond more positively to elements that follow the Golden Ratio. I also believe that, because this ratio is a part of our innate inner nature, the recognition of it triggers our Chi to make us feel better and have a positive response. It *feels* familiar.

Later, a man by the name of Leonardo Fibonacci discovered the unique properties of numbers multiplied and how they frequently showcased a consistent but unusual phenomenon found in the natural world. He coined this observation the Fibonacci sequence. How original!

The Fibonacci sequence starts with a one or a zero, followed by a one, and proceeds based on the rule that each number (called a Fibonacci number) is equal to the sum of the preceding two numbers. For example, F (0) = 0, 1, 1, 2, 3, 5, 8, 13, 21, 34. This mathematical sequence ties directly into the Golden Ratio. The idea is if you take any two successive Fibonacci numbers, their ratio is very close to the Golden Ratio. As the numbers get higher, the ratio becomes even closer to 1.618, the Golden Ratio. For example, the ratio of 3 to 5 is 1.666. But the ratio of 13 to 21 is 1.625.

Now if this makes your head hurt, I get it. A mathematician, I am not. But, these numbers can be applied to the proportions of a rectangle, called the Golden rectangle. And since we are talking about the mysticism to Shape in our homes and how that energy affects our life, it's time to wake up for those in the back of the room napping.

The Golden rectangle is considered one of the most visually satisfying of all geometric forms, hence, the appearance of the Golden rectangle found throughout architecture. The Golden rectangle is also related to the Golden spiral, which is created by making adjacent squares of Fibonacci dimensions. For our purposes here, we don't need to learn math. However, the Golden Ratio has been used to achieve balance, harmony, and beauty within and around our spaces for millennia. Studies have shown that when test subjects view various buildings, people, and art, the ones they deem most attractive and appealing are those with solid parallels to the Golden Ratio. It's important to note, these were subjects that were just average people unaware of this principle, but the Golden ratio elicited an instinctual reaction every time.

THE SHAPE OF CHI

As previously discussed in earlier chapters, there are many factors that affect the course of our life, but none are as important as Chi. Chi is the energy that produces and maintains lakes and streams, mountains and hills, trees and plants, and all of the natural world. It's also what carries you, your thoughts, and your actions. If the veins of your environmental Chi are kinked or blocked, Feng Shui is required to refine and smooth the energy to enrich your Chi.

If the Chi in your environment is trapped due to a poor shape, it can affect the way the Chi carries your body, the way it feels, how you move, and even how you speak. Several years ago, I had a home in the shape of an ice skate and the client was perpetually spinning in different directions. Another home in the shape of a cleaver suggested danger and violence, causing slumped Chi and anxiety.

Now, not every home has a literal shape to it, but this is where reading the Chi and honoring your first inspiration is key. What is the first thing that comes to you? Does it hold the Golden Ratio, making it appealing and pleasing? Or does it hold "something" that you can't put your finger on? If Chi cannot circulate properly, it will incapacitate your life over time. Typically, as Professor Lin often stated, it will show up within three to five years of living in your home. If your personal Chi is incredibly strong, it may take longer, but no matter what, if Chi is strangulated, negatively altered, or paralyzed in any way, it will show up in your life. And remember, without Chi we cease to exist.

Chi is different in every area and every home. It is a living, breathing entity unique to each home and plot of land. The shape of your land and home either contributes to healthy, meandering Chi or it kinks it. It's never neutral. If the Chi in your environment is deterred or crippled in any way, your body and life will reflect it. Chi literally determines if you will have a happy, positive experience or a dull and frustrating one. And don't forget, your Chi carries emotions and feelings within your personal Wi-Fi, and if it's not healthy, it will attract the same.

Ideally, you want balanced Chi that smoothly and easily flows through a home, both upstairs and down. If the home has a hindering shape, the immediate goal is to untangle the energy to prevent knots from showing up in your life. Ultimately, the Chi of a home affects its atmosphere and if not cared for it will trickle down to its occupants. Think about various places you've been in your life and consider some of the homes you've lived in. Think about the experiences that showed up while living in certain homes. Some spaces feel lively and comfortable, happy and homey. I liken this to a warm hug. But some places are cold even in the dead of summer, feel dull, and you can't shake off a feeling of being sad and sluggish. These are all characteristics of house Chi. Bottom line is this; when you enhance the Chi of your home, you improve the Chi in yourself.

To me, the shape of a home is essential in evaluating house Chi. By reviewing the shape of a home, you can better discern how Chi is circulating and if it has a positive or negative pulse. If the shape is challenging, an occupant's chances for health, wealth, and luck are dramatically reduced. If the shape is really challenging, life will become greatly imbalanced and arduous.

Imagine flying above your home and getting a bird's-eye view of its shape. Is it square, rectangular, or shaped like a T, U or an L? Most homes fall into one of these five shapes. And it's important to note, anything that is attached to the main house is apart of its shape, including garages, additions, and screened-in porches. Not only is the overall shape a clue to a homes' house Chi, but so is the application of the Bagua Map that we discussed from Chapter 3. Starting at the front entrance, or mouth of Chi, use this vantage point to set the map over your entire home. This helps determine the orientation for the whole building and reveals where certain life areas may have kinks. The map is always placed at the front of the home, even if you use a side door, the back door or the garage door, the front door is always the starting point. Whatever the shape of your home, fit the layout inside the Bagua Map so that the nine life sections are laid out over your home.

If your home is an L, T or U, there will be parts of the map that are outside the shape of your home. If the home is square or rectangular it is considered a whole shape, perhaps helping us to get closer to that Golden Ratio. If you have small projections like bay windows, fireplaces, or other pop outs, they act as energy enhancements. Much like an added bonus! But if there are areas that are recessed, indented or completely missing, those are life areas where energy is kinked and house Chi will be affected.

The shape of your home literally sculpts your life, and over time can dramatically shift your Chi like water dripping on a stone. With shear awareness even an amateur can identify to some degree that when energy is missing or kinked in some way it's going to influence your life.

In many ways Feng Shui is its own Golden Ratio because it's a divine language filled with ancient myths and symbols that are unexplainable, and mysterious, yet proven to work. From ancient times to now, however, experts have utilized Feng Shui to study and interpret signs, symbols, and shapes to reach genuine illumination on how the unseen effects us. Hidden in the shape of your home are whispers to your psyche. We not only mirror our environments but they mirror us. Your home is not an inanimate box of floors, walls, and rooms. Its overall shape, shapes you. Like a symbiotic relationship, Shape determines how you react, respond, and develop daily habits. Consciously and subconsciously, overall Shape takes on great meaning in all of our lives.

RECTANGULAR AND SQUARE

Many man-made shapes have been taken to the extreme for the sake of art, but rarely is an establishment developed for healthy Chi. In Feng Shui, whether we are assessing a room, an entire floor, apartment, or home, the ideal shape is square or rectangular. This is considered not only appealing but it feels good. A rectangular or square shape also portrays a solid foundation for which one can build fortune and luck.

In ancient times, the traditional Chinese home was placed in what's called the arm chair position. With a hill or mountain behind the home, this provided the energy of the tortoise, tiger, phoenix, and dragon for safety, protection, and luck. Later, homes were built to house an interior court to infuse the home with the vital Chi of nature, but it was also symbolic of the geometric reflection of mountain energy, which upon closer look, instinctively introduced occupants to the Golden Ratio.

L- AND T-SHAPED HOMES

This is a common home shape in the West, but it poses many problems. Because this shape is incomplete, many occupants will find themselves saying they feel stuck, things aren't working, or things are lacking. It's important to note, in both the L- and U-shaped homes, the placement of the kitchen, master bedroom, and the dining room are particularly critical in determining the fate of the occupants. If these rooms are located in the front of the house, it's like having your private matters on public display and can cause marriage and friend-ship instability.

Those who are aware of Feng Shui principles avoid L- and T-shaped homes. They are evidence that some area of life will be missing and cause instability. An L-shaped home can be a challenging one to live in if the Feng Shui is not healed. The repercussions can range from minor disorder and interruption, to major health issues, loss of resources, or even divorce. Growing up, one of my dear friends lived in an L-shaped home. Her parents argued all the time and the entire family battled many health issues. Throughout high school, my friend had her mouth wired shut from a baseball accident, battled strep throat numerous times, and broke her leg twice. We used to laugh at her bad luck, but as I got older and started learning more about this mystical tool, I realized it was her Feng Shui!

A T-shaped home poses many of the same challenges because an area of the home is extended out of proportion. Traditionally the extension is towards the back. This can lead to heart issues, lack of good judgment, or infamy. In rare cases, the middle portion of the T is at the front of the house. Depending on proportions, it could have an auspicious nature, however, in most cases, it poses restricted Chi and partners arguing about money.

The good news is, if you live in an L- or T-shaped home, there's no need to panic. It can be easily healed from the outside with landscap-ing, using a fountain, lights, or trees. Or you can heal it from the inside of your home with a faceted crystal ball or mirror.

For an exterior application, simply place a tree, light, or fountain in the area that would complete the home's shape into a square or rectangle.

If you live in an apartment or condo with no outside access, or you don't want to heal the Feng Shui with landscape, use a faceted crystal or a mirror. For an interior application, simply hang a crystal in the window or a mirror on the wall to symbolically push out the wall and recapture the rectangular or square shape. The goal is always to achieve a solid, stable shape.

U SHAPE HOME

Another common shape in the West, the U shape typically has the entrance inside the U and the Chinese refer to this as a Chinese Locke House, because occupants are energetically locked out. This can be considered highly unlucky for marriage. Once again, if the kitchen, owner's suite, or dining room are located in the wings of the U, this can cause instability in a marriage, cause friends to never show up, and literally leave someone locked out. In addition, the occupants may battle chronic health issues, career ups and downs, and constant struggle. I have yet to see a home with this shape that isn't experiencing at least one, if not all, of these issues.

In the course of my career, I have seen many U-shaped homes, but one in particular stands out. Many who follow my work are familiar with this story because I share it often, and even I was shocked by its results! The results so mystical and magical, in fact, that it quickly became a service that everyone was asking for because it proved the power of Feng Shui.

In 2016, I looked at a home and I was immediately drawn to its U shape. The mom had just had a baby and was struggling. The owner's suite was located partially in one of the wings of the U shape, leaving the bed symbolically halfway in and halfway out of the house. Literally split down the middle. I asked which side of the bed the mom slept on because I had a premonition that she was struggling in this house, and if she slept on the side that was "out," she most definitely was struggling. Intuitively, I felt like she was managing everything, but feeling "locked out." Literally, I felt her voice was unheard and she was struggling to speak up about what she really needed, and she was about to fall apart.

Everything I saw in the plan was exactly what she was experiencing. Her husband wasn't listening to her, and she always felt left out trying to manage everything on her own. Essentially, she was a single mom living with a roommate. I'll never forget the day I went to her home to heal the Feng Shui. While she was at work, I had asked her husband to take their young child out of the home, along with the two large dogs so I could perform my ceremonies. Everything you can imagine going wrong, went wrong that day. The front door had a digital keypad on it that malfunctioned and chirped loudly the entire time I was there. I unwittingly removed some clothes out of a sink, and ended up with baby diarrhea running down my arms and all over my clothes. The husband, who was supposed to leave for a minimum of two hours, returned after thirty minutes with two large dogs and a screaming one year old. Chaos ensued for the next two hours. Despite encountering what felt like total anarchy, I did my best to perform the ceremonies, shift the energy, and heal this house's Chi. When I left, I was exasperated and exhausted, but mostly deflated and defeated.

When I got back to my office, I immediately called my Feng Shui teacher in tears. I felt like I had failed my client, and I needed my teacher's wisdom to root me back into reality so I could figure out what to do next. And that's exactly what she did. In fact, her advice floored me and has never left me.

"...Your client is a struggling mom who has the weight of the world on her shoulders. She is unable to speak up, and the more she does, the closer she gets to falling apart. Her luck has diminished, she's exhausted, and she is unable to ask for help. Your experience today was the house speaking to you, letting you know what she feels trying to hold it together for the family and showing you what the mom is experiencing every day. This was a gift, not a failure."

Not even two hours later, I received a call from the client. She was screaming into the phone, her voice filled with tears. Her husband had sat down with her that night at the kitchen table, something he never did, and proceeded to tell her he had been a terrible husband and father and, moving forward, he was going to step up and be a better man. This would later become known as "The Harper Experience." From logical thinking, it can seem impossible that a house has the ability to speak, that she has a language. Over the years, I have encountered dialect from many homes. Whether it be my first home, BoBo, Barbara's home in the woods, Harper's, or countless others, each has a colloquial language to share.

Like the T and L shape, you can also heal a U-shaped home through its exterior. Place landscaping outside the home to repair the U shape and turn it into a square or rectangle. Plants, shrubs or trees can all be an excellent choice. Another highly effective and profoundly spiritual adjustment is to use red string or red string lights. Run it around the perimeter of the home to complete its shape. This is what I used with Harper's home, and the proof is in the pudding!

If possible, avoid having the owner's suite at the front of the house. The front of the home is an active yang space. The front of the home is an area ideal for activity, not privacy. Instead, use it for the children, a guest room, or an office. If it's unavoidable, place a mirror in an adjacent room to transcendentally pull the relationship back into the house. Do the same if it's a kitchen or dining room. While most would consider those yang activities, they represent the heart of a home's energy. Cooking and dining are an intimate experience that require mindfulness and slowing down for better fulfillment and enjoyment. Such a sacred activity cannot energetically feel like it's "going out the door."

THE SPIRITUAL SIDE OF SHAPE

Shapes are the building blocks to everything we see and experience. Even with a loss of sight, an object's shape resonates to touch and vibration. It is fundamentally how we interpret the world. It is God's thumbprint to convey emotional resonance in a nonverbal way. It is either harmonious or discordant, and it can always be felt. Through auspicious shape, we can experience a sense of order and connection to all that is.

In Feng Shui, shape determines how you experience your environment, how it touches your soul. Even if it can't be seen, it can always be felt. The shape of your environment shapes you. It shapes how your Chi finds joy or undergoes suffering. Look closely at the shapes that surround you, because they unknowingly affect you. Many of my clients have lived in ill-shaped homes, clueless to how that energy changed their Chi, but immediately experienced a shift when they got it right. The recognition doesn't always come easily, but if you're willing to go on a mystical Feng Shui journey, you'll mature to an understanding from first-hand experience!

EXERCISE

TRACING THE NINE STARS

How to bless your home

This is a mystical exercise to bless and activate Chi. In addition, this is an excellent ceremony when your environment or life needs a method to rid your space of bad luck. It is also a great tool for blessing a new home. This is a very transcendental technique and requires a strong spiritual practice of daily Chi cultivation to wield energy in a powerful way. Nothing is required other than knowing the Nine Star sequence. Due to the spiritual nature of this exercise, it can be done at a distance even when you are unable to physically visit. Perhaps someone is sick, or in another country. All you have to have is your cultivated Chi and the Nine Star method. Its purpose is to purify, cleanse, and move Chi, and transform the energy to feel more positive and uplifted.

According to H.H. Professor Lin, we are often covered in "worldly dust." Before performing this exercise, it is important to sweep away this dust to clear away anything in the way of your authentic self. For example, dust may include unfaithfulness, cheating, dishonesty, guilt, etc. Remove these obstacles by cultivating your Chi and practicing meditation to improve your power. The following is a guideline to remove "wordly dust" and start this method.

- Visualize a pink lotus flower with eight petals blooming in your heart space. This is where your Buddha nature resides. This is your authentic self. Visualize the blossom as a sparkling crystal that is as bright as the sun, and the light fills your entire body.
- See your heart merging with that of Buddha's heart, and your mind merging with Buddha's mind. See your true Buddha nature coming forward, free from worldly dust.
- Visualize this light filling your entire body with Buddha's wisdom, including your head and heart. His spiritual power fills you up and together you are one.

- If you are physically at a space, begin the ceremony immediately upon entering. If you are doing this remotely, skip to the next step.

- Placing palms in a prayer position, recite this mantra nine times: Gatay Gatay, Para Gatay, Para Sam Gatay, Bodhi Swaha. This is known as the Calming Heart Mantra.
- Imagine 10,000 Buddhas filling your body with their light and essence. You must draw on this power to cleanse the space. If you skip this step, it pulls from your personal Chi and will quickly deplete you.
- Move through the space either physically or energetically according to the numbers on the floor plan, known as the Nine Star path.
- As you move through the space, either physically or energetically, project light above and below, through the walls, and all the way out to the exterior. If your spiritual nature is strong, this will be easy to do.
- As you move through the space, visualize that you are removing all obstacles and difficulties, any sickness, or negativity.
- After cleansing each point, send blessings, and envision that all nine spaces are cleansed and emanate nothing but positive blessings. Visualize purity, love, and light.
- When I have reached the ninth point and have sent purity, love, and light to all spaces, I seal my practice by reciting the calming heart method again. I also thank all the deities, gods, and Buddha for helping me in this ceremony.

During this ceremony, you may gain insights about yourself or your space. Listen carefully. Feel into it. This is a time to reflect about questions you have about your space or your life, and they may be answered during this ceremony. Pay attention to insights and always honor your first inspiration before logic sets in. Write them down, and write down how you feel before and after. Reflect on your experiences and continue to listen throughout the next couple of days, especially in your meditation practice. Your insight can become pure gold!

10

KNIFE-EDGE

...be prepared to give up every preconceived notion, follow humbly, wherever and to whatever abyss Nature leads, or you shall learn nothing.
  T.H. Huxley

$\mathscr{F}$eng Shui originated in ancient China. It was a tool developed to help create positive energy for residences, tombs, government, temples, and palaces. Because the concept of Feng Shui has been around so long in this region, it is deeply engrained in its history and tradition, so much so that few question its ideologies. Most who use it firmly believe that Feng Shui expels negativity and invites in auspicious Chi, as well as increases luck, health, and wealth. Through exploration and experimentation over the course of millennia, various regions of China came up with methods for overcoming difficulties based on experience, folklore, and local beliefs. In fact, they took the spiritual nature of such decisions very seriously. Everything was taken into consideration and nothing left out. The wind, rivers, earth, sun, trees, and more—it all mattered.

They reviewed the best way to construct buildings by following the way, or Tao, of Nature, honoring her Chi and learning to speak her language to peacefully coexist. They would choose the best plot of land, observe how the waters flowed, document annual rain amounts, monitor the wind, and, with reverence, use their knowledge to improve the harmony of inhabitants to live in harmony with the land. They even explored invocation, the use of spells, and other mystical tools from the local shamans to solve all problems that lie within the mystical realm of the unseen. As a result, ancient wisdom has been woven into the fiber of modern times to help everyone improve their living spaces with a tool called Feng Shui.

Realistically, everyone has used some form of energy work to achieve a positive result in their life, even if they didn't call it Feng Shui. Despite this, many still see it as a superstition or voodoo. And it's understandable. From a visible aspect, it's easy to investigate the truths behind Feng Shui ideologies and agree. For example, it's easy to recognize dilapidated Chi when you visit a run down home. Or how problems might arise when a front door works improperly. You can see it, you can *touch* it, and more importantly, you can explain it. So maybe this Feng Shui stuff is real? However, when you enter into the world of the unknown and unseen, it can challenge your limited beliefs, and the ego, and make you quickly put Feng Shui right back into the box categorized as "superstition." No other concept in Feng Shui can challenge your beliefs more than the theory behind the knife-edge. On one hand, it makes perfect sense and on the other hand it seems downright nonsensical. The only way to truly compre-hend it is to develop a relationship with your Chi and the environ-ment you live in and, rather than think your way through it with reason, you arrive at it through *feeling*. A knife-edge is an unpleasant experience that you may not have known what it was, but you can feel the difference when something has changed it. Even though all of the five disruptors I share in this book have a mystical aspect, many have a tangible, physical thread that helps you take the leap of acceptance. Like the trusting lamb, you see a small safety net of familiarity that you pull from the recesses of your mind and accept a shred of belief. But the concept of the knife-edge could challenge everything you've known, at least until you reflect on a time where you tried to sit near one, or sleep near one, and realize you *felt* it.

WHAT EXACTLY IS A KNIFE-EDGE?

In the simplest of terms, a knife-edge is any sharp point directed at you or your home. And just like commanding your power, it's really important to focus on your bed, desk, and stove area to avoid what's commonly known as "sharp shooting Chi." From an exterior standpoint, points can be generated by features such as sharp roof lines, the corners of homes, large buildings in close proximity, large ridges or boulders, or any other sharp protruding object that appears harsh. This is especially important if you have a point directed at your front door which commonly occurs with pillars. From an interior standpoint, a knife-edge could be produced by a wall corner, sculpture, overhead soffit, pillar, or piece of furniture, the most common being a wall corner or ceiling edge.

Diagnosing the affects of a knife-edge is a matter of judgement and can easily be shoved aside for other things in your life. But if an edge is pointed at you its effects are potent. Not surprising, if left unaddressed and not adjusted, a knife-edge can have very negative consequences.

A couple of years ago, I worked with a client by the name of Jessica. She had a large knife-edge in her bedroom that was extremely close to her bed. It was located right at her shins when she laid in bed. I asked her if she found sleep difficult or had any leg issues? In fact, she did. So much so that she switched sides with her husband, and then he developed issues. Oftentimes the only way we can truly believe a concept is to experience it first hand. After experiencing restless leg syndrome and insomnia, Jessica had chalked it up to other factors in her life. She had a new baby, and work was hectic, so these issues had to be stress related, right? Unfortunately, this isn't a concept we can logically explain our way through and call "stress." It has to be felt, and as soon as Jessica adjusted the knife-edge both she and her husband never had issues again.

Knife-edges are considered inauspicious because they are similar to sharp knives, or pointing fingers. They threaten you and bring harm by undercutting your Chi. If a knife-edge is in an area you spend a lot of time in, it will lead to conflict. They can cause nervous issues, indecision, restlessness, and can result in many health issues. Now, imagine if a bed is out of command and has a knife-edge from a nearby wall, do you think this person will have the ability to stand in their all-knowing power? Most likely, they will not. It is only by coexisting with your environment that one can truly achieve peace and harmony.

...for the last several decades a remarkable body of evidence has accrued suggesting that our current understanding of reality, the solid and comforting sticks-and-stones picture of the world we all learned in high school science, is wrong.
Michael Talbot, pg. 5, The Holographic Universe

INCREASING DISCERNMENT

Using meditation, doing spiritual cultivation daily, and adjusting your environment with Feng Shui allows you to experiment with the energy around you. Through cultivation, you will significantly influence how you *feel* spaces, and it will increase your relationship with your environment. Ultimately, by experiencing the significance of wielding energy to achieve a more positive Chi flow, you increase your wisdom and spiritual instincts. You cultivate the ability to discern how the unseen may be affecting you. You heighten your awareness so you can *feel* beyond the visible world. Much of our lives is based on hope when it should be based on faith. Hope lacks certainty; faith is absolute trust in all that is, even if you can't see it or explain it, because you can feel it. With the entire cosmos running through your veins, you have the ability to tap into your power and knowingness and understand that the invisible world is far more than what you have perceived. Without faith, you fall into skepticism and fear. You rely too much on what is known and what you think is certain. With faith, you have no fear and accept that the unseen is where subtle, powerful frequency resides.

When ordinary elements like a wall edge can transform you into another dimension, through feeling frequency, you jump from everyday chaos to touching the primordial light of the cosmos. This is the magic of Feng Shui. It opens up a sixth sense and gives you a glimpse behind the curtain, allowing you to experience something new. No matter your level of faith, if you can drop your preconceived notions and limiting perspective, practicing Feng Shui brings you closer to God. Inch by holy inch, the fundamentals of energy bring mystical experiences into your daily cultivation and expand your belief. Learning about knife-edges and their side effects can leave you teetering on the edge of belief only in physical matter, with staunch notion that frequency doesn't exist, or it wakes you up to other-worldly aspects of an invisible microcosm. The choice is always yours. Feng Shui is a spiritual practice founded on personal experience. Only when you can experience the affects of "sharp shooting Chi" can you embrace that there's more to this than what's perceived by the naked eye.

THE ILLUSION OF MATTER

Physics is the foundation for all of science. And despite the astounding leaps in the field of quantum physics, many scientists are still stuck in the very tidy ideology of Newtonian approaches on how the world works. It's clean and simple and easy for the 3D ego mind to accept and explain. It sticks to the physical, tangible world and it ignores the quantum, unseen world where matter is actually made up of energy and there are no absolutes. In fact, at the atomic level, matter doesn't even exist, at least not with certainty. But the Newtonian approach is orderly and elegant, and it's reassuring to an exact mind. Sounds like oscillating science focusing on outdated ideologies that fluff an existing limited belief system, but I digress!

For years, scientists have denounced practices that involved energy. Psychic phenomena, spontaneous healing, Feng Shui, paranormal activity, acupuncture, astrology, prayer, reiki—this is the work of charlatans because it defies the Newtonian philosophy of absolutes. Essentially, if you can't see it, it doesn't exist. Energy modalities of any kind have been demonized for centuries because they were not tied to a traditional belief system and failed to show reasonable proof. From *The Biology of Belief,* by Dr. Bruce Lipton, he writes on page 87,

> "In 1893, the chairman of the physics department at Harvard University warned students there was no need for new Ph.D's in physics because science had established that the Universe is a "matter machine" made up of physical, individual atoms that fully obey the laws of Newtonian Mechanics."

The idea of a knife-edge is controversial. It is a thought-provoking idea that challenges the traditional Newtonian outlook of cold hard facts. With little experimental evidence to go on other than feeling it first hand, how can the concept of what it is, and how it behaves be explained? With little to no formal research, most avenues to explain knife-edges have been severely distorted and its importance obscured through skepticism and pessimism. Why? Because science is not as objective as we would like to believe.

We view scientists with a bit of awe, and we respect their intelligence, so we are convinced that their ideologies must be true. In fact, when I think of my grandparents, they never questioned their doctor's prognosis. They wholeheartedly believed he was the expert, and the thought never occurred to them that he could be wrong. Yet we forget that scientists have the same religious, philosophical, and cultural prejudices as the rest of us. And let's not forget, there is a great deal of evidence that the Universe embodies considerably more than our world view allows. But it has only been in the last ten to fifteen years that I have seen a growing number of people abandon the ideology that what they are being told is truth. More and more people are standing in their power and seeking new opinions and learning to create a better reality. By stepping into your power, you change your vibration, emitting a new frequency. Perhaps the most important consideration in understanding a knife-edge is not about trying to explain it, or make sense of it at all, but rather understand how it makes us *feel*. It's not a visible, tangible thing that can be put into a Newtonian box, but it's a feeling that everyone can describe. The clue to the puzzle that started it all was based on feelings of agitation, restlessness and anxiety. Could it be that that the ancient mystics were right, and a knife-edge does in fact, have "shooting Chi?" Upon further review, it turns out it does. A sharp corner or edge has been shown to hold a different frequency!

SO WHAT EXACTLY IS FREQUENCY?

According to the Britannica dictionary, "In the most general sense, frequency is defined as the number of times an event occurs per unit of time. Or the number of cycles or vibrations undergone during one unit of time." In other words, frequency is the number of energy waves that pass a fixed point, like a knife-edge, in a certain amount of time.

According to existing research, the human body as a whole has a natural frequency of about 7.5 Hz, but different body parts, like the heart have a frequency of 5 Hz. The head and spine have relatively higher frequencies of 8-12 Hz because it is said that depending on the degree of flexibility or rigidity, muscular tissue being more flexible, like that of the heart, or bone being more rigid, like that of the spine, each produces different waves. A study done in 2018 by Hindawi, called the Journal of Sensors, expresses this. It was a study done on the vibrational characteristics of human comfort in special equipment cabs. They found that the equipment's vibration and frequency over long periods of time would affect the urinary, digestive, nervous, and cardiovascular systems, leading to health issues. They found that, in order to protect the drivers physically and mentally, they had to control the vehicle's vibrations and the frequencies emitted from equipment within a reasonable range. They learned that, in order to avoid body issues, they needed to control several factors to improve the natural frequency in the range of 6-8 Hz. Through further study, they discovered that the EMG and EEG energies could reach 10 Hz to 20 Hz, and this caused the skeletal muscles to contract. They found that the equipment regularly ran at 12 Hz during normal working conditions. Therefore, the frequencies were disrupting the head and spine.

Several studies have been done to learn the effects of vibration and frequency on the body from equipment, trains, airplanes, and vehicles. They have learned that it causes back pain, bone damage, heart conditions, digestive issues, respiratory issues, pain, and more. According to the workers' union of Australia, the longer a worker is exposed, the greater the risk of health effects and muscular disorders. Despite numerous studies done for workers' unions, and the health of workers, little has been explored in the way of sharp objects, like knife-edges. While writing this book, I reached out to several physicists asking for their comments on the possibility of "sharp shooting Chi." Most did not respond, but the one that did said, "It's an interesting topic, one that should be explored further, but it's of little interest to me personally."

The physical effects of frequency and vibration can be severe. Studies have shown that dynamite blasts and even large aircraft can contribute to low-frequency building vibration and can induce building damage. If it can damage a building, then what is it doing to its inhabitants? Another controversial frequency-producing machine is cell phones. Cell phones are said to emit a frequency of 900-1800 MHz and many articles and studies have shown that exposure to electromagnetic fields may affect brain physiology and cause other health issues. But who's to argue about a device that all of us are tethered to?

Another non-physical war that has been going on around the unseen is the radiation emitted by electrical smart meters and wireless devices attached to homes. Even the traditional energy meters placed on every home to provide it electricity emits a low frequency. However, many argue that the newer smart meters, replacing the old ones, produce up to sixty times more radio frequency radiation than the traditional devices. But many corporations, especially electrical companies, are swift to undermine the sheer thought that they could be hazardous to our health. Regardless, it's hard to argue when so many people who have entire building panels outside their window suddenly get brain tumors or other types of cancers. Once again, if we can't see it, how can it possibly affect us?

My dear friend Libby lost her niece to EMF, or electromagnetic frequency, from an electrical grid that was placed right outside her bedroom. Both her bedroom and her school had high levels of EMF, and her little system couldn't process it. Due to this tragic incidence, and Libby's own sensitivity, she fights to educate people on the unseen effects of EMF today. Libby experienced it first hand in her medical office and said she felt like she was going crazy. She described herself as buzzing, and she felt like she was crawling out of her skin. In the middle of Chicago winters, she found herself lying in the snow to connect to the earth to find equilibrium. It wasn't until she realized the enormous amount of medical equipment in her office, emitting copious amounts of EMF, that was making her feel this way. It was affecting her system. Only after removing all the equipment was she able to produce an environment that made her feel normal again.

Many people, myself included, are highly sensitive to their environments. People exposed to EMF report feeling tired, achy, foggy headed, nauseous, or like they are buzzing when they are in an environment with high amounts. In extreme cases, a person can find it impossible to function, or develop severe side effects like brain cancer. With so many unseen things in our world altering our bodily functions, is it impossible to think that a sharp edge could do the same? I leave its efficacy up to you.

We cannot see gravity or Wi-Fi, and yet we aren't all floating around, at least not yet, and our devices magically work. We can't see wind, and yet we've all felt it. Each of us, at one point or another, has experienced an anomaly and chalked it up to something that could be logically explained. And yet, more than half of you have likely been affected not by something seen, but by something unseen and been changed by it. I have experienced the unseen effects of a knife-edge firsthand. I find it impossible to sleep when a knife-edge is coming at my bed. In times when I have tried to work with a nearby knife-edge, I find myself restless and can't focus. In my own practice, I have seen all sorts of ill effects from people trying to work, sleep, or cook near a knife-edge.

I've seen entire businesses fail due to an adjacent building pointing a large cutting roof line right at them. I've seen homes experience strife, strained family dynamics, arguing, and more when an adjacent home's Chi came shooting at their front door. Is it all in our heads? I'll let you be the judge, but I think it's safe to say, it's time to break free of our illusions around matter and realize we need to expand our world views beyond an outdated Newtonian belief system.

SO WHAT ARE YOU GONNA DO ABOUT IT?

Of all the adjustments available in Feng Shui, the knife-edge is the most fun to remedy. It requires creativity and experimentation. Because a knife-edge emits a frequency, each of us responds to those wavelengths differently. The best way to alter that frequency is to soften the edge. Traditionally, an edge would be changed or softened by a plant or a faceted crystal. But I always encourage students of Feng Shui to explore and have fun with it. There are no hard and fast rules when it comes to healing a sharp corner in your home or office. The only rule that applies is that you change the frequency. In the past, I've used custom pom-poms on a string down the edge. I've had long strips of leather placed on a hook to be hung on an edge as a decorative art piece. I've used rounded molding, fabric, ribbons, scarves, and I have even tried beads! The sky is the limit. Get creative and have fun with it, and if one option doesn't feel great, experiment with something else. For exteriors, you can place a concave mirror over your front door to push the negative Chi away.

THE SPIRITUAL SIDE OF A KNIFE-EDGE

The ancient Chinese art of acupuncture teaches that every organ and bone is connected to a meridian point, or energy point, in the body.

By activating these points, through the use of needles or pressure, the Chinese believe that energy imbalances and disease can be corrected, and that many chronic ills can be alleviated and cured. The body has over a thousand meridians, and even though it cannot be seen, its results can be *felt*. In the fall of 2021, I started seeing a Chinese medicine doctor who specializes in acupuncture. By evaluating the Chi from my blood pressure, eyes, and tongue she knew that I had inflammation in my gut. She encouraged me to get a colonoscopy, but until that day came, I went to her every week to work on digestion and the gut biome. Within weeks of seeing her, I had more energy, faster responses to healing, and better sleep. Feng Shui is similar. I evaluate a home's Chi. I look at her energy points, starting with The Top Five Disruptors™, and determine how to release pressure, move energy, and alleviate issues. Most of what a practitioner does is through her intuition. It's the immediate inspiration of what the home is saying to her, not physically showing her. And it's how it all feels.

Science is rarely a force that offers us solutions to the world of the unknown or unexplained. In order to do so, it must revaluate its objectivity. There are compelling reasons to go beyond what we can explain, and yet it can still be met with ridicule. It has had a tendency to accept what is probable if the matter of study was considered acceptable, and if it's not acceptable, it falls into the category of "Charlatan's work or snake oil" and it's unacceptable and mocked. Until science can overcome its shortcomings and its double standards can be eliminated, we cannot make significant strides in spiritual phenomena. And as long as the unknown remains frightening and unexplainable, I'm afraid we'll continue to remain in a very dense existence. Luckily, as humanity continues to awaken, we are learning how to be a part of the solution, and we are realizing that we can abandon outdated ways of thought and be proactive in choosing a new way of being.

To discover new ways to think about our reality, and more importantly, feel our reality, perhaps we no longer rely on science at all and what it tells us, and instead we, the people, forge a new path for evolution. By revisiting ancient wisdom, and instead of stripping it of what fits into our current belief systems, we return to its intelligence with reverence. By tuning into the wisdom of the local shamans we can indeed solve all problems that lie within the mystical realm of the unseen, and gain better understanding of "sharp shooting Chi." Clearly, they were much further up the mountain than any of us have been.

EXERCISE

MEDITATION

Meditation is not about spending thirty minutes a day to carve out of your busy day to sit and stare at a wall or the back of your eyelids. It is about spending time to think about what you desire and what you need to create right now. This is a place to expand and dream and think of all that is possible. Slowing your thoughts down to a manageable, more easy pace so that you can cultivate your Chi and connect yourself through the cosmic mind.

If you allow it, meditation will be your greatest gift to yourself. When turned into a daily ritual, you'll find yourself missing it if you skip it. Whether you take the time to journal, contemplate, sit quietly, walk in nature, or visualize some far off place by reading, it's a time to allow your mind to play, relax, and wander. It is not a time for your mind to be squashed and overwhelmed with worry, to-do's, and deadlines.

The art of meditation is about "being" rather than "doing." Many people who take the time to meditate find it easier to make decisions and they often get "downloads." Their demeanor is softer, and they find that they move through situations with ease. Plus, cultivating a meditation practice gives your Chi a spiritual resonance that reverberates throughout your environment.

As your practice grows, so will your abilities, and you'll fine tune your instrument to awaken dormant instincts. Inner vision and hearing will improve, but most importantly, your sense of feeling at peace will increase. As your vibration increases, so does the health of your Chi and, after a few months, a new level of contentment and happiness will bubble up. Let's all meditate!

Meditation is a great way to cultivate your Chi and heighten your senses. Choose a time every day that works for you. Doing this in the morning can change your life, but if it's easier, do it in the evening before bed. Creating a loose habit makes it easier to place in your schedule so you honor it and make it happen.

- It only takes fifteen to thirty minutes. Sit quietly and just breathe. Take these minutes for yourself to get clear and gain clarity for the day. You can close your eyes or reflect quietly with them open.
- Keep a journal with you to jot down notes. I find that a lot of info rushes in when I get silent. Put it down on paper and get it out of your head.
- Segment intending. In the book, *The Law of Attraction,* by Ester Hicks, she has a section that talks about intending each segment of your day. Rather than focusing on the ten things you will be doing this week, it teaches you to focus, fully, on what is in front of you right now. I love this practice because it keeps you present in the Now moment. Try doing this for a week and see what happens!
- Breathing. We aren't talking short sips of air here, I'm talking nice, slow deep breaths, that get down into your belly. It is said that one minute of deep, slow breathing can pull anyone out of an anxiety attack, so slow down and bask in relaxation.
- Set a timer. If you are constantly stopping your process by

looking at the clock, set a timer so you can focus on your practice.

- If you have a tendency to fidget or you can't sit still, use what is called an "anchor." When I first learned how to meditate, my instructor taught me to anchor my thoughts on two things. Doing a full-body scan— my toes, my feet, my ankles, all the way up to the top of my head, and he taught me to focus on the breath going in and out of my nose. You can also press each finger pad into your thumb, over and over again.

- Another great tool is Mantra. In Chapter 6, I shared the mantra, So Hum. This is an excellent mantra to start with. Sit quietly and simply repeat over and over.

- Give yourself at least a week to incorporate this new practice into your lifestyle. Take notes on how you feel when you start, and how you feel after seven days.

11

BATHROOMS

"Our spiritual value is not dependent on pleasing some conceptual God. It is the result of the way we harmonize our yin and yang energies."
I Ching

My Feng Shui teacher, Katherine, who studied under Professor Lin for twenty-five years, used to talk about how Professor Lin wanted someone to write a book about the five senses. I have yet to find a book on the subject that goes into great depths, and I find this quite curious since the five senses are what makes us human. They help narrate how we perceive the world, how we uniquely experience it, and how we make decisions based on them.

While I have yet to find or write a book about the five senses, there is no place in the home that touches the five senses more intimately than our bathrooms. It's where we go first thing in the morning after our nightly slumber, with sleepy eyes, groggy thoughts, and little mobility to try and wake up. It's where we eliminate what our body no longer sees useful, and it's where we can be seen as most vulnerable. We come face to face with sweet and not so sweet smells, visually see ourselves come to life in the mirror and touch our skin delicately, the sounds of running water and flushing toilets in the background. No one room is more rousing to our five senses than the bathroom. Teetering on the spectrum between disappointment and pure delight, we experience it all in our bathrooms. As I write this chapter, I personally have never spent more time in the bathroom than these past months. In late 2021, I was diagnosed with Crohn's disease. I've spent many days on the bathroom floor, tracing the lines of imperfection in my baseboards, seeing the tear in the left cabinet door, and noticing the crooked installation of the flooring that I had missed for the past three years. Yes, this is an intimate experience.

When I was thirteen, I had my first kiss in a bathroom. It was with a boy named Marvin. His last name escapes me, but the girlish delight and elation I had to have my first kiss was far more important than the details of a dirty, unkept bathroom. As my adult mind thinks back to the state of that gross bathroom, my sense of smell and touch are overwhelmed with disgust, and yet my childhood memory is nothing short of amazement from that experience. Hindsight is twenty/twenty.

When I was twenty-one, I went to the bathroom while on a date. I wasn't sure it was working out, and to my surprise when I returned to the table there was a one carat diamond ring and a proposal for marriage. *Man, I need to go to the bathroom more often*, I thought!

Through sickness and in health, this space observes our hurts, our bruises, traumas, and dramas. It notes the gray hair and fine lines that grow over time. But it also witnesses the joy and excitement before a first date, or the thirtieth wedding anniversary dinner. It envelops us in elation when we learn a little one is on the way, and reflects back to us all our hard work from six months at the gym. It absorbs our deepest thoughts, our innermost ideas and puts relaxation in motion after a long day, and it sees our most intimate grooming habits. This space sees, feels, hears, tastes, and touches all the senses.

SETTING THE INTENTION FOR A HEALTHIER BATHROOM

Energy adjustment practices are very important when it comes to your bathrooms. This area represents emotion, health, and finances, and can quickly deteriorate an important life area depending on where it lands in your home. Bathrooms pose a problem because of how they alter and move valuable Chi. Rather than allowing Chi to flow gently, it's forced up and down violently by moving water and drains that inhale it. Whether it's being flushed away by a toilet or forced down the drain via a shower or faucet, it is forced to move quickly. In addition, the average bathroom now has three to five drains in it. Chi is not given the chance to easily meander through this space, but rather it's engulfed.

Due to the proclivity of bathrooms being negative, over the years many clients have believed that changing their life experiences could only occur by altering their home by remodeling it, fearing that the only way to stop negative Chi would be to move the bathroom to another area of the house. I blame much of this on scary information out there regarding Feng Shui that puts people in such a tail spin of fear. Rather than empowering people to wield and manipulate the energy and coexist in harmony with their environments, many teachers educate people on all the things that can go wrong, so who can blame people for freaking out? I've seen so many books and articles written about bathrooms being negative and have seen some calling it the "devil's room." Good God! Here's the thing to remember about this seeming inauspicious space in your home: Your most powerful weapon or tool in combatting a bathroom's fast-moving Chi is you. But your personal Chi and your inner environment needs to be cultivated so that you can manipulate your external environment in a powerful way. This creates a potent combination that is highly effective and far less expensive than moving the bathroom down the hall! As you've learned, Feng Shui requires you to work in two realms, the visible and the invisible, but the strongest lesson is belief in your ability to heal it yourself, and telling that energy where to go!

A bathroom's main purpose is to remove waste, so it carries

connotations of impurities. And our world is obsessed with cleanliness. We wash away dirt and grime with soap and water. We wash away the day during a hot shower, and we eliminate our own waste by way of the toilet. Despite being a Feng Shui nuisance, it is a modern-day convenience many of us greatly appreciate. When addressing a bathroom, the main intention is to keep healthy Chi circulating and do everything you can to prevent it from constantly going down the drain. Another key objective is to keep the intimate parts of the bathroom from circulating around the house. For example, keeping the unsavory parts like sights, odors, sounds, and so on from invading other parts of the house. Alas, this does not mean our bathrooms are doomed. The goal is to minimize the issues by using your powerful energy tools to make your bathrooms healthier and stronger.

LOCATION, LOCATION, LOCATION

Bathrooms drain vital energy from a space. Of all the places in a home that bathrooms can be located, the hardest on an occupant's life is in the center of a home. The reason this becomes an issue is because this area of the home is the center, it is the heart of all things and touches all areas of your life. Imagine if your own heart had a hole in it. It would wreak havoc on your whole body. Having a bathroom in the center of your home ultimately depletes all your life areas, creating a slow leak that harms everything in your life. It can represent an enormous loss of resources on all fronts. I see a lot of powder rooms tucked into this area of homes. While this makes its location convenient for access from all areas of the home, it negatively affects you and other occupants. It will not only drain finances, but this can also be the hardest on your health!

Another area to avoid is a bathroom at the front entrance. This seems like an odd place for a toilet but I have seen this countless times in my own practice. More recently, I visited a brand new home where the entry was exactly opposite the powder room. Six feet away from the front door was the toilet. In fact, if the front door was open, the neighbors could see the toilet! As you've learned from Chapter 8, the front door is very important. This is where all vital Chi enters your home. Having a bathroom located here significantly drains the incoming Chi that could be entering your entire home. It's like eating food and then spitting it out. Since this area involves change, how you think, connecting with the outer world and your career, having a bathroom here will affect many areas of your life.

Five years ago, I had a woman reach out to me with this same detail. The bathroom was not only in the center of the home but the toilet was just a few feet away from the front door. I asked her if she had any issues with her health or career. Indeed, she did. She had countless jobs and found it difficult to keep them because her health was getting worse. I found out she had thyroid cancer. This was an instance where remodeling was in order. It is rare that I recommend such an extreme adjustment. But with her weakened state and declining health, she was not in a position to wield energy in a powerful way. So she hired a contractor and moved the bathroom door to another wall. Within eight months of doing this, her health improved and she found a job she loves.

Humans possess a propensity for wanting and accumulating more money. And from our current state of reality, why wouldn't we? It provides us an increased sense of well-being knowing that we have enough, and it provides us the almighty sense of security that we are taken care of. When our finances are strong, we have an easier disposition. It's easier for us to focus and find joy in our lives because our basic needs can be met. Due to a culture raised on mass consumption and a susceptibility to always wanting more, it's easy for humans to get into the aptitude of not having enough. It can feel like money is coming in and going right back out. And if that is the case, it could be your Feng Shui is adding to the stress. During my personal apocalypse, or what I like to call the Dark Ages of Amanda, almost all of my homes had an inauspicious, or negative, bathroom location in the back left corner of my house. This is a vital energy center that represents acquiring, keeping, and having money. A bathroom in this area can "drain" your funds, creating constant unexpected financial issues. Likewise, this area also represents the element of wind. So if the back left area of your home is compromised by a bathroom you may find yourself distracted and not listening.

Other than the three placements within the home that can be harder to work with, I find that the bathroom layout tends to be the most problematic. The layout is always dependent on the placement of the toilet, or the king of all drains. When you enter the bathroom is the toilet the first thing you see? This can have negative effects on your health, especially those that involve the digestive tract, and this is another design detail I see a lot. Rather than placing a beautiful vanity as the focal point, many homes have the throne front and center. This isn't desirable, because subconsciously you're constantly reminded of what the toilet represents: waste and elimination. This can drain your Chi over time. Bathrooms are indicative of many spiritual representations but toilets are closely linked to the bodies internal plumbing. Leaks, malfunctions, or odd placements can lead to constipation, cramps, and other other digestive issues. Furthermore, be mindful of the overall size of the bathroom. This is especially important for the owner's ensuite that often comes with expansive rooms for grooming. An oversized bathroom is said to lead to vanity and over primping, and can cause an obsession with cleanliness, while a small bathroom that feels cramped can cause restrictions and health issues.

WAYS TO ENHANCE BATHROOM CHI

From a design perspective, I feel that color is especially important in a space that is as intimate as a bathroom. You need to feel safe and secure, and no other tool can do that like color. Color affects how we feel, so I typically choose colors that are soothing, like blues or greens. Most importantly, choose colors that make you feel less stressed and anxious so it's easy to create a peaceful mood. It has become very popular in recent years for bathrooms to be all white. While this does overcompensate for the feeling and sense of cleanliness and purity, over time this can feel depleting. Our Chi must have color to feel uplifted and elevated. If you prefer a white backdrop, accents are a terrific way to boost a space with a little personality. Towels, artwork, mats, and other accessories can quickly add just the needed pop to bring your bathroom alive.

The bathroom is a place to enhance and boost your five senses. It is a place that you can bring your Chi to rest and collect yourself. The Chinese believe that a clean and beautiful bathroom keeps a household happy and healthy. I couldn't agree more with this philosophy. Of all the rooms in the house, this one space explores our five senses the most and, if we allow it, has the potential to give us an enormous amount of healing. Add beautiful colors, calm music, and soft towels. Use high quality toothpastes and mouthwashes that you really enjoy and consider having beautiful candles or incense on hand with delicious smells. When our five senses are peaked with delightful sensations, our Chi is fluffed and happy. This creates valuable energy deposits to have in your space to lift it up. Use this space as an incubator to recharge. Taoists believe that the nutrition we receive from air alone is more valuable than food. As we inhale, we draw in valuable, vital Chi. As we exhale we release, cleanse, and detoxify. The art of breathing can be overlooked during a hectic day. The Chinese consider deep breathing a necessary health regime to practice daily.

By doing this, you internally balance yin and yang, correcting your personal Chi flow. In acupuncture, it is thought that illness occurs when the correct Chi flow is not maintained and Chi becomes unhealthy. Use your time in the bathroom as a sanctuary for slowing down, breathing deeper, and stimulating all five senses.

NURTURING YOUR BATHROOM

No matter where your bathroom is located or how it is laid out, Feng Shui always has an option to heal it. Since the goal in a bathroom is to keep healthy Chi from going down the drain, your intention when adjusting it is to reduce the draining effects it has. If your bathroom is located at the front door, in the center or in the back left corner of your home, keep the door shut and place an over-the-door mirror on the exterior of the bathroom door. In addition, use color to your benefit. Green can represent growth and vitality, and increase well-being. Yellow is an excellent color for a bathroom located in the center because it promotes health and a strong heart. Black serves as a color of wisdom, and is great for a career. Blue can represent new beginnings and make a space feel fresh. Believe it or not, despite the popularity of grey in many bathrooms, the Chinese believe it denotes frustration and hopelessness, so I tend to avoid it. If you prefer a more neutral option, opt for white or cream.

Mirrors, often called the aspirin of Feng Shui, are another great tool. They lift, push, expel, and expand Chi. If you have a bathroom in a poor location, or a poor layout, traditionally practitioners would place a small round mirror on the ceiling above the toilet to pull Chi back up. If your health is very poor and you are unable to spend time cultivating your Chi, this may be an adjustment to do for thirty to sixty days to boost needed Chi. Use of a small 3" diameter ceiling mirror is a powerful way to wield energy back up if doubt doesn't get in the way. I've suggested this adjustment to clients and some can't get over the aesthetics of it. Despite it being small and unnoticeable, if this is not an adjustment you want to try, another option is hanging a faceted crystal from the ceiling between the vanity and toilet. This, too, lifts Chi back up and is very inconspicuous. To kick it up a notch, hang it by red string. In extreme cases, another trick is to place mirrors on all four walls. I personally get dizzy with this adjustment but if you have a powder room in the center of your home and life feels like its out of control, go to extremes to get the energy right. Soon enough, we will all be able to see these subtle energies that mystics have spoken about for ages and ages and realize what fools we've been!

THE SPIRITUAL SIDE OF BATHROOMS

A bathroom is not a place merely for cleaning oneself. In fact, in many cultures and religions, ablutions, or bathing rituals, have symbolic meanings and ritualistic powers. For example, healing for Buddhists it not about curing the body, but a bathroom involves transforming the mind and soul. In all Buddhists texts, Indian, Chinese, and Japanese, the mind is the source for all suffering. Therefore, health and healing have always been understood to be mental and physical; they cannot be separate. To cleanse the body is to cleanse the mind.

In Islam the hammam, or Turkish communal bath, is a womb-like space where Muslims spiritually purify themselves before entering a mosque or reciting the Koran. It is a space described as an epilogue to the flesh and a prologue for prayer, where the sacred and profane come together.

Historically, the Greek and Roman baths were less about hygiene and more about ritual bathing to nourish the mind and body for civic life.

In Feng Shui, our bathrooms are a necessary space to improve our lives, despite connotations of negativity. Not only do they improve convenience, but they also cleanse the mind, body, and spirit. They allow our Chi to come to rest. But this can only occur if the energy is balanced and cared for. This space has the ability to rejuvenate us, replenish us, and fill us up. While we may not be a part of communal ritualistic bathing for spiritual purposes, we all have the ability to reconnect to our beingness via this space. Through linking the sensations of the mind, body, and spirit, this in essence is what ritual is all about. Just like lighting a candle or kneeling to pray, bathing your soul is about imbuing this space with your own spiritual meaning. And if the belief that dunking in a river to become baptized can wash away original sin, imagine what can be achieved by invoking your personal watering hole with spiritual matter. Indeed, a bathroom can become a spiritual experience.

EXERCISE

COLOR AND ITS MEANING

I am so thankful for design school and learning Feng Shui. It has allowed me to create spaces that are energetically valuable but also pretty. Color is always my go-to trick to enhance any space quickly. By choosing the right color for you and your home, it imbues it with personality, a certain mood, and changing the Chi. Here are a few colors and their Feng Shui associations.

- Pink is a color many of us know. It represents love, softness, and purity. It also stands for joy, happiness, and romance. Besides its meaning, pink is an absolutely beautiful color for a bathroom.
- Red represents fire, happiness, and strength. In Feng Shui, red is a power color. It is known to create energy, promotes positive Chi and good luck, and expels anything negative.
- Peach suggests romance and attraction.
- Orange signifies happiness and power. In addition, in many cultures, orange represents friendliness.

- Yellow expresses tolerance, perspective, and loyalty. It is also the color for strong health.
- Green represents new beginnings, hope, and growth.
- Aqua, or blue-green, denotes positive beginnings, spring, and nature blossoming.
- Blue can represent new beginnings, spring, and hope. In old traditions this was used as a secondary mourning color, and it is sometimes avoided. However, many modern traditions have abandoned this theory.
- Purple and deep red are very auspicious and signify nobility, power, and richness.
- Black or dark colors invoke wisdom and intellectual depth, but use sparingly as too much is evidence of depression and lack of hope
- Tan or beige connotes new possibilities. It is said that after one endures disappointment, they find success. Tan symbolizes this theory.
- Brown represents stability, like the roots of a tree. It has long-lasting and enduring qualities, elegance, and sturdiness. It is also said that it represents the passage of time.

Colors set the tone for your environment. Great care should be given to the choices you make to create certain feelings and moods. If the color is right, your space will feel welcoming and warm. If it's wrong, it could feel jarring and off. This effects the Chi. Whether you place these colors in your bathroom or throughout your home, be mindful of the energy you set forth for that space and make sure it feels appropriate. There is no right or wrong, but always be sure to sense its effects and how it makes you feel.

THE SHIFT

"Less and less do you need to force things, until finally you arrive at non-action. When nothing is done, nothing is left undone."
Tao Te Ching

For over twenty years, I have been asked hundreds of times about the nature of Feng Shui. What is it? How exactly is it different from decorating a house? What are the benefits of it? Why should I even consider doing it? Is this shooey stuff even real? These questions are all based from the root of an ego mind trying to make sense of the unknown.

In the context of asking questions, it seems innocent enough. Should I, or should I not take this Shui stuff seriously? However, these have not been easy questions to answer. Albeit the closer we have come to the shift, the easier it has gotten. Or perhaps that's just the old age talking, and answers come from a place of compassion rather than frustration. Either way, the truth is, we have entered into a new era of energy medicine. In 2012, many thought the world was coming to an end, and in many ways it has. The old world that is. We are evolving into a new way of being and redefining our understanding of ourselves and the world we live in. No longer do we reside in a 3D ego world where everything fits in a nice, elegant, Newtonian box. Very soon, we will know ourselves far beyond the five senses and emerge as multi-sensory beings, rendering many of our old thoughts, behaviors, and beliefs obsolete. We will move past speculation and skepticism about whether our emotions and vibration have creative power. No, in fact we will come to know this as absolute fact. Healing will reach far beyond the allopathic system and encompass energy modalities as everyday practice. There will be a return to herbs, sound, and light, because only they can hold the vibration of true healing. Our environments will become cohesive parts of our "being-ness," and within the very walls of our spaces will be healing frequencies that improve our well-being. The old adage that illness can be systematically improved by synthetic drugs and synthetic means, and that the home environment is separate from one's healing will become seen as harmful rather than beneficial, and be the old way that is outdated.

WHAT IS THE SHIFT?

A massive shift is occurring as the human race up-levels from a 3rd dimensional reality and into a 5th dimensional awareness. What does this mean? It means we are entering into an age where we abandon the belief that thought and mind are superior to the heart. That instead, we will shift to knowing by vibration and feeling not by reason and thought alone as we have for millennia. A massive holistic movement is upon us as more people wake up and embrace a new realization of self. That within us all lies the keys to the Universe. We've just been too asleep to realize it.

A dimensional shift is essentially when a cosmic body, like planet Earth, moves from one dimension into another. The entire planet and her inhabitants will experience this shift. The Native Americans believe we are moving from a fourth world to a fifth world, a change preceded by a day they call The Day of Purification.

As someone who has been a part of the holistic and alternative world for over twenty years, I find this new shift full of possibility. In my early days, much of my work was met with ridicule and mocked for being weird. But a new consciousness is being birthed and it's one filled with exciting new ways of being. I have met more people in the last five years wanting to know more about energy, and how to create a holistic environment from the inside out than in all my years of practice. I am excited and confident that this book serves as a guide to help people on their journey home.

WHY DOES THIS SHIFT MATTER?

As I look back over the years of growth and change, it seems unwise not to acknowledge that we are emerging into a new world where energetics will shape all of our lives for the better. I believe that, as more people rise in their evolution, their hearts will open to serve humanity in ways we never expected. Our children will grow up only to know sustainability, kindness, and equality. We are finally moving at a pace that brings humanity to wholeness as opposed to living a life filled with greed, corruption, and selfish behavior. Thought and fear has driven our patriarchal world for far too long. Now it's time we recognize the importance of empathy, compassion, and community by leading with the heart and allowing the Divine feminine in all of us to rise.

I invite all of you to explore and research how the invisible world of the planet also includes intricate grids of energy that affect how you feel. The geomagnetic field is weakening, the frequency of the Earth is changing, known as the Schumann Resonance, and this is healing us and changing how we think. In the future, these grids will act as beneficial aids in keeping us healthy and happy. In fact, everything in our world will aid in healing us.

Using the principles of energy, we will be renewed and all our needs met with everything in our daily lives, optimizing our bodies natural capacities. Cell phones, computers, appliances, our homes, cars—as the technology progresses and our awareness expands everything in our world—will aid in healing us with powerful, beneficial frequencies, not depleting us or affecting us in adverse ways as they did in the past. Nothing in our world will deplete us. Nothing will be produced that compromises the integrity of our health or our beautiful planet and her inhabitants.

Buddha, Mother Mary, Lao-tsu, Jesus, Abraham, Krishna, Babjji, Mohammad, and thousands of other great masters have been our greatest teachers of eternal light. That the key to our very existence lies in remembering our greatest gift, and that's love. Each of us has this great intelligence and wisdom deep within us, and once this becomes clear, that it is our thoughts, feelings, and emotions that are key, we can pass through the cosmos and go from one existence to another.

RELEASING FEAR AND EXPECTATION

Wherever there is wisdom and compassion, we come to the male energy. Wherever there is love and truth, we find unity through the female energy. These yin and yang energy states are what become the most valuable possessions you can have when transcending to the higher world of creation and oneness. There is no way to physically prepare. There is nothing to do. You do not have to earn your way to the higher world or prove your worth. You are all guaranteed this beautiful and exciting journey because you are all a part of all that is. Collecting food, burying your goods in the backyard, or amassing money will not serve you. In the higher worlds, you are what you create energetically. If you prepare on a physical level, it will not serve you because the dimensional shift takes you into an entirely new energy, a new consciousness of different creation where no physical preparation can help you. Success depends on spiritual awareness and belief in your beingness. This isn't a place, but a vibration.

There will be very little violence approaching this shift. This is the perfection of life that we have created through the collective mind. While it is debatable how long this will unfold, many believe that is will occur over the next five to seven years. However, because this is an experience, a vibration, and not a place, I think each individual will shift at their perfect timing. I have a strong sense that my greatest leap will occur in four years. And I would be remiss if I did not mention the children of our planet. I have said for years that the children who have entered this planet over the last twenty years are what created the anomaly of higher consciousness, a quickening of sorts, to help this transition be easier and smoother.

Unlike us old folks with 1985 DOS computing software or older, the new children coming in have a higher consciousness and are holding more light. They are the ones with the DNA upgrades and fancier software making this incredible shift possible. They are the leading edge of consciousness. Vast numbers of children with high spiritual awareness have come to Earth, helping us transition and transcend to a higher vibration. How is this possible? In addition to different DNA, a child's pure innocence and high levels of love and compassion are what make it possible for us to connect to the harmonic level of creation itself, that of love.

HOW DO YOU KNOW IF YOU'RE SHIFTING?

What does this higher realm look like? How will we get there? How do I know when I've shifted? What about my family? Honestly, we 3D humans are very funny creatures. Incredibly exciting things can happen all around us, and not only would we rationalize them with our minds, but we'd most likely miss them from the trivial nonsense we consider important. We do everything we can to keep our little realities comfortable and unchanged because to do otherwise is something to fear or might make us uncomfortable. We love to know ahead of time what to expect, and we want to know the outcome. We want to control the journey. Some may want to stay asleep and ignore the many awesome changes that have improved our daily lives, especially those from the past one hundred years. Think about the enormous amount of change our world has received in just a matter of a century. Imagine going back to the 1700s and trying to explain our world to their primitive civilization, and yet not much changed for hundreds of years until suddenly we had the industrial revolution. It's no accident that technology has accelerated and advanced the way that it has. Edgar Cayce, Nostradamus, Yogananda, Mother Mary, the Bible, and many others predicted a time of great change. Some saw it as destructive with an unrecognizable Earth, and others saw it as a time of immense spiritual awakening. I'd argue that it is absolutely a time of immense spiritual growth, making our 3D world unrecognizable, so in many ways it's both. But it's time to let go, surrender, and allow. Be in awe of all that has changed.

For me personally, the greatest shift has occurred over the past ten years. For you, it may look different. The timing of it all doesn't really matter. What matters is how small shifts in your behavior have brought you closer to who you truly are. Instead of judging yourself for not being spiritual enough or not feeling or seeing any changes and thinking this 5D shift is complete bologna, let's first look at who you are in this Now moment. How do you respond if a friend or family member upsets you? Do they trigger you in the same way they did ten years ago? If so, how quickly are you able to move through that energy? Have you noticed a higher level of compassion for people around you, even those you don't know? How interested are you in matters of the heart like equality for all, world peace, and eliminating the injustices of what we are doing to our planet and each other?

I've noticed an enormous level of compassion grow in my heart in the past decade. I am far more open to letting people know how I feel, and sharing my love and appreciation. I make it a point to always let people know they matter. I give, I share, and I fight for injustices that I feel are worth fighting for. People who are no longer of this vibration have fallen out of my life. Recognize that the people and friends you have in your life now are likely not the same as you had ten years ago. As you grow and shift, so does your vibration, and that affects what you attract into your life. It also changes what you are willing and not willing to tolerate in your energy.

WHAT ABOUT THE PLANET, ANIMALS, AND NATURE?

Everything in our world is making the shift, including our beloved planet, nature, and the animal kingdom. As mentioned before, anything not of integrity, like synthetics that harm us, will fall away. Nature, as she continues to elevate, will produce herbal remedies far more powerful than anything we've ever known in the medical community. There will be a return to herbalists and healing through nature. Animals will also make the shift, and many already have. Notice a difference in their behaviors and how they are aiding you in your transitions. Also recognize more visits from wild animals in nature. They are speaking to you in spiritual language, so listen to her whispers; they are there to guide you.

Utilize nature to help maintain your higher frequencies and ground you. She is always speaking to you, but you have trained yourself to listen to other things outside yourself, like news outlets, social media, people, or parents. Don't value words or actions of other things; value feelings and vibration and your inner truth, because that is where we are headed. Let this information inspire you, not limit you. It is your words, the vibration you emit, your level of compassion, and your ability to listen through your feelings that puts you back in communication with the expansive world within you. You've lost touch with the light of the Universe within you, and this is how you begin to reconnect.

BREAKING THROUGH ILLUSIONS OF TIME, SECURITY, AND HEALTH

There can be many side effects during this shift, like headaches, joint pain, fatigue, nausea, and auto immune diseases as the body transcends. Learn to slow down and simplify. Everything in our reality is made up of frequency, and as you transcend, your body will eliminate what it does not need and appear to break down. It's an illusion. Imagine yourself as the chrysalis. The old must go away for the butterfly to emerge.

Everything we've come to know in our world as safety, security, and stability will change. Time itself will no longer be linear but expansive, and it will bend. Much of our power has been given away to clocks and calendars. We've even gone as far as deeming some things more appropriate simply due to a time of day or a time of year. We will break free of this illusion and learn that all we have is this Now moment. The ideology that we are running out of time, or something has to be done by a certain time frame, puts us into a very constricted state and disrupts our ability to freely create. And we will become less and less concerned about where we are at, where we are headed, or how we might get there. All attributes of the ego mind trying to keep everything under control. Instead, be willing to cut all ties to outcomes, expectations, and people. Let go of all attachments.

The shift is not about doing, but instead about being, embracing how you feel right now, what you'd like to do right now, how you'd like to create right now. And that is all there is in the *isness*. Right now. So how on Earth do we have or make any commitments with no time? I can't fully describe it, but it will be about being on the same frequencies, vibrational matches that link us up.

We are already getting glimpses of this new way of existing without time thanks to new generations busting through the old belief systems and structural paradigms, old systems put in place since the industrial revolution that no longer serve us. The younger generations demand less structure and honor their Now moments by wanting to work when it benefits them. This is not laziness. This is changing how we view work and the lack of balance we've accepted for the last century. Work, and fast-paced, high-strung, lifestyles have been the norm. We have accepted that work is more important than our personal lives, putting our work schedules as the main priority. And we have glorified a hectic, crazy schedule as a badge of honor.

More and more work places are realizing that the younger generations don't work this way. They literally aren't built for it. Their software is much different and they are here to show us how to bring balance back into our lives. Companies like Uber, Shipt, and other businesses that operate through apps and flexible schedules, allowing people to earn a living on their own terms and what fits into their personal life, is how work will continue to evolve. Autonomy, independence, and valuing freedom is all apart of the shift.

FREQUENCY AND VIBRATION ARE THE NEW VERNACULAR

If you haven't gathered, frequency and vibration are the currency of the fifth dimensional world. This can be a hard concept to embrace while still living in a five sensory world. However, we are making the shift to becoming multi-sensory. Many are gaining new abilities and getting to see past the veil. We are inundated by frequencies on a daily basis, like those from a knife-edge, but our instincts have been so dulled it's been hard to measure it accurately without a questioning mind getting in the way. Moving ahead, frequencies will become more apparent and carry far more weight than the things we have deemed as safe and secure in our physically dense world. Your frequency and the frequencies around you become a barometer for how to communicate with your reality.

Currently, you're experiencing and bumping into frequencies and vibrations all day but don't even realize it. Luckily, this denser reality is coming to an end. Each of us will come to recognize not only the signature frequency that we hold ourselves, but the frequencies that others hold, along with the frequencies from objects, our environments, cities and all the things around us. The exciting thing is that when we develop the ability to sense the frequencies around us, we will have far more power than anything we've ever experienced in the physical form.

There is still so much to evolve and be discovered in the aspects of frequencies. It's easy to jump to the conclusions that humans will use this as a tool to get what they want and use it for the wrong reasons, but with a higher awareness, we will come to know this as the way to connect to the secrets of the Universe, and it brings us back to love.

Many of you are already starting to feel this and have been deemed "sensitive." In the past, this has been to your detriment. Many empaths are overwhelmed by their level of receptivity to the energies around them, myself included. As a sensitive, you are more open to energy and better able to discern subtle energy vibrations. On a subconscious level, this is what can be felt near a knife-edge, or being out of command. But now these abilities are becoming a prized asset. Hone them and cherish them, as this is the language we are moving into.

SURRENDER AND LET GO

Nothing is to be forced or pushed. That is the old way. It's time to surrender, simplify, and allow the expansion to occur and unfold naturally. Desire is the whisper in your ear. Creation occurs when you let go and give in to the circumstances so you can move through them and arrive at a new consciousness. The desire itself is the accelerant. The desire is what summons new frequencies, and this is how you grant yourself the ability to communicate, manifest, and create.

We live in a world that exists only from the constructs of collective consciousness. This is what Michael Talbot described in his book, *The Holographic Universe*. It is only light, and we are of that light. We are all children of God, which expresses through us and speaks to us through love, joy, and happiness. The yin and the yang, we create it all. Within all of us a great potential so vast that if we combined all the adjectives in the dictionary we could not describe *it* with justice. But we can all feel it. We all have been given a great gift, and that is the gift of free will, or choice. You can continue on your path, trying to accumulate more things, making your life more comfortable, trying to control things through force, and making more money. But the external world is not something to usurp, rather it's an opportunity for you to go within, see the contrast of what doesn't fulfill you, and remember to see God who expresses in everything through joy and love. Come to realize that the inner and outer world both reside within you. That is where Heaven and Earth collide and connect you to your soul. That is the yin and yang of all there is. Open your heart fearlessly to the unknown and see God in all things, but most importantly see and feel God in you.

13

UNVEILING

"We delight in the beauty of the butterfly, but rarely admit the changes it has gone through to achieve that beauty."
Maya Angelou

When I look back at all my amazing years on this planet, I know without a shadow of a doubt that I would not change anything. Despite all the trials and tribulations, and the ups and downs, each crossroad has lead me to where I am today. Each experience gave me the opportunity to choose a path and shape a beautiful thing called life. Even when I look back on some of my hardest, darkest days I know that it made me who I am today. Difficult experiences make you stretch and expand to find your soul. Each step up the mountain gave me higher wisdom and greater perspective. That is what creates the unveiling to a deeper, more meaningful life.

After moving to Nashville, I lost touch with Marlene but later learned she had passed away. I also never saw Barbara again after her home was completed, but I will never forget that day in the woods and how that pivotal time changed my life. About a year ago, I had lunch with Jane. It had been eight years since I had seen her. I shared my story with her about that time in my life and thanked her. That experience was my dark night of the soul. It forced me to reflect, expand, contract, fall apart, and like the Phoenix, it showed me how to burn it all down and rise again. Feng Shui is a tool that can lead you down a smooth paved road, and somehow, if you listen to its wisdom, you end up on a narrow gravel path up a mountain. Each person that comes into our lives is there to teach us something and help us grow. When I look back over my life, there are countless people that have emerged to show me a better way of being. Some visit for just a few short hours and others are lifelong companions going up the mountain with me. Regardless of time, each one is meaningful and filled with purpose.

I began my career in traditional science because I believed that logic was the key to contemporary success, not to mention respect from my peers. After a synchronistic meeting with a strange woman in a bookstore, I am now filled with the realization that Feng Shui was my path all along. My degree in traditional sciences simply gave me the necessary backdrop to expand my mind into Eastern philosophy and provide me proof that the unseen is far more powerful. Unwittingly, many of us intuit holistic practices everyday, synchronicities that romance you down the rabbit hole to remind you of things that simply have been forgotten. The way we treat buildings, nature, and each other is instinctively hardwired into our brains. It all comes back to love. However, due to mass skepticism and poor conditioning, we tend to get stuck in a dark backdrop instead of opening ourselves courageously to the infinite cosmos.

The study and practice of this mystical tool has taken me on a fantastical adventure, discovering immeasurable possibility and illumination. From the start, this captivating ideology opened up many doors of curiosity deep in my soul and, although it started a bit frivolous and simplistic, the search has never ceased to amaze me. It has gone far deeper than I ever imagined. In my opinion, Feng Shui has been oversimplified to quick measures and, *voilà*, you'll achieve a lifetime of health, wealth, and happiness. Honestly, with such promises, who could resist the shallow expectation of such hope, especially in an instant gratification world? But upon deeper investigation, this tool is far more profound than most realize. Not to mention, its incredible ability to show us fortuity if we choose to see it. It has the ability to open your heart and expand you to a level of understanding you never thought possible. Listen to her wisdom.

My twenty-year journey has taken me into the realm of folklore, symbolism, mysticism, and ancient wisdom beyond this reality, and I'm still learning. Although you may want to simplify it for sheer convenience and ease, understanding the principles of cosmic breath through mystic tools like Feng Shui can help you accelerate your unveiling of self, layer by holy layer, exposing deeper truths. Entire fortunes have been lost, marriages have fallen apart, and unexpected poor health has occurred to those who refuse to acknowledge the unseen. But to each her own on their path up the steep mountain called enlightenment. It's a different view for everyone.

Chi is everything and everything is Chi. Learn to draw from this Universal principle for your benefit and learn how to work with it. Learn how to understand her frequencies. Feng Shui is a wellspring of opportunity that can give you an expanded vision of all that is possible. Every day, we dance in and out of spiritual and intellectual consciousness, searching for ways to be more present and mindful to maintain a harmonic mind, body, soul connection. Why not do more of it by practicing Feng Shui?

By witnessing Feng Shui, you learn that consciousness evolves every day, and through a lifelong study of experimentation, you co-create your existence. Regardless of your age, ability, or apparent intellect, anyone, including you, has the power to perform energy work like Feng Shui. And with great success! All that is necessary is a zest for life and vitality of spirit that emanates positive energy. This is creation at its most primal level. With an open heart and mind, a daily practice, and optimism, you will continue to lift the veil of ignorance and reveal so much more. Your environment is a metaphor reflecting back to you the beauty and dynamic nature of your Chi and surrounding reality. Feng Shui helps you piece together a large puzzle one section at a time, helping you create a continuous narrative of your expression of existence, all through the beauty of energetics.

Let this be a manifesto for a new generation of seekers. What I've learned for sure is that for most, enlightenment takes a lifetime to achieve, if not lifetimes. Few will experience it all at once. For most, it is a slow unveiling over time, like an oak tree sprouting from the earth, taking years to grow her wings into the sky. Look for the answers all around you, especially in nature. I find that nature gives me clues to understanding this gift called life with sacred reverence, continually giving her wisdom asking nothing in return. Each day will be different. One day, you may be swimming in bliss and experiencing samadhi. The next may be filled with self-realizations loaded with false truths and human frustrations. Every day, you'll be faced with the ignorance of this world. It truly can be an undertaking filled with emotional hazard.

But as you rise, those emotional hazards are turning into your greatest asset, a new language. Each day, you feel different, and will be different, and so will your Chi. What you put into your mind, body, and spirit materializes in your Chi and manifests in your life. This greatly affects the flow of your Chi, so make sure the energetic consumption is positive. Practicing Feng Shui and experiencing its magical dance is the moment the individual self and the universal self merge. This is the divine dance of the miraculous. This is not a practice to be done once and deemed complete. For the fruit of Feng Shui to emerge is a refining process each and every day, because you yourself are being refined, too. Your search and curiosity should continue.

Together in unity, we will elevate to another world. How can this be possible? The first shift starts with you. You are the one who inhabits the greatest gift and that is the vessel of your current incarnation. Use it wisely. Care for it and care for its vibration. You have the power to heal yourself and others just through raising your vibration. And rather than wondering how others think or what their agendas are, come to know all that is through *feeling* your way into it. Marvel at the idea that our world is changing. As energies stream through your body, in and around you, your mind, body, and soul connects exquisitely to all that is. Feel your environments changing too.

The use of energy is safe, it's all-natural, and it's free. And it's becoming the way all matters are organized without ridicule or question. Energy is becoming our medicine. Medical institutions will change in the future. Healthcare as we know it will die, leaving only small portions as we currently know them in place. Only through light, sound, and frequency will our bodies and environments heal, as the old way will not be able to vibrate at the higher levels. Those energies are connected too densely to the 3D world of power, greed, and manipulation.

Your soul is the source for all of your energy. It is uniquely your own and has a signature as unique as you are. The soul is the manifestation of the all-pervasive intelligent energy of creation that locks in the vital mysteries of our existence that we have forgotten. But through empathy, love, and compassion, we tap into the great ocean we have all come from and we are remembering its fingerprint. When all of our energies, from our personal energy to the energy of those around us and the energy of our environments, are brought cohesively together, then together we will come into 5D harmony. And together we will flourish, because this is the soil of the soul.

INSPIRATIONALS

We have a tendency to think in terms of doing
    and not in terms of being.
    We think that when we are not doing anything
    we are wasting our time.

But this is not true.
    Our time is first of all
    For us to be.

To be what? To be alive, to be peaceful,
    to be joyful, to be loving.
    And that is,
    what the world needs most.

Thich Nhat Hanh

INSPIRATIONALS

When your world moves too fast
    And you lose yourself in the chaos,
    Introduce yourself to each
    color of the sunset.
    Reacquaint yourself with the earth
    beneath your feet.
    Thank the air that surrounds you
    with every breath you take.
    Find yourself in
    the appreciation of life.

Christy Ann Martine

ACKNOWLEDGMENTS

Thank you to Amy Wray. You are a wild, creative soul and my life would be less than without you. Thank you to Sharita Star for always providing me guidance, love, patience, and a sounding board when I need it most. Thank you to Deborah Stillwell for years of incredible friendship, guidance, and teaching me proper grammar, which I'm still working on, but I will get there! Thank you to all the amazing guests that I have had on the Home | Energy | Design podcast. You've been a light and a force that proves we have the ability to change the world through intelligent conversation. Thank you to all my clients over the past twenty plus years. Not only do your stories splash these pages, but each experience led me to be the practitioner I am today. Mr. Lagana, we've had our fair share of ups and downs, but at the end of the day it led to deep respect and friendship. Thank you for all of your help over the years. And finally, Melissa Cooke, you have provided me great joy and humor, much-needed guidance but most importantly, incredible friendship. Thank you.

RESOURCES

Bibliography Notes

I Ching, Book of Changes. Hua-Ching Ni. 1983

The Diamond Cutter, Geshe Michael Roach and Lama Christie McNally. 2009

Homes that heal, Athena Thompson. 2004

Interior Design with Feng Shui, Sarah Rossbach. 2000

Ancient Secret of the flower of life, Drunvalo Melchizedek. 1994

Living in a Mindful Universe, Even Alexander and Karen Newell. 2017

Anatomy of the Spirit, Caroline Myss. 1996

Taoism and the Rite to cosmic renewal, Michael Saso. 1972

Feng Shui, The Chinese Dragon. Lillian Too. 1993

Big Magic, Elizabeth Gilbert. 2015

The Divine Matrix, Greg Braden. 2007

From Deep Space with Love, Mike Dooley and Tracy Farquhar. 2017

Anna, The voice of the Magdalenes, Claire Heartsong. 2010

Feng Shui revealed, R.D Chin.1998

The Tao of Physics, Fritjof Capra. 1991

The sacred and the profane, Mircea Eliade. 1968

Folk Religion in Southwest China, David Crockett Graham. 1967

Heaven and Earth and man, Helmut Wilhelm. 1977

Waking up in 5D, Maureen J St. Germain. 2017

Frequency, Penny Pierce. 2009

The Law of Attraction the basics of teachings of Abraham, Esther and Jerry Hicks. 2006

The Everything Essential Buddhism Book, Arnie Kozak. 2015

Between Heaven and Earth, Harriet Beinfield and Efrem Korngold. 1991

On Life after Death, Elisabeth Kubler-Ross. 1991

ADDITIONAL RESOURCES

I'm thrilled that you're joining me on this Feng Shui journey! After reading this book, you now understand how to achieve a happy, healthy, home™ using Feng Shui principles, and how to have a kick-butt relationship with your home.

If you want to learn more, be sure to check out my website, podcast, and online courses. I have a ton of helpful resources to help you continue your spiritual adventure!

Website: Gates Interior Design
   https://gatesinteriordesign.com

Podcast on iTunes: Home | Energy | Design
   https://podcasts.apple.com/us/podcast/home-energy-design/id505550006

Videos: Amanda Gates Feng Shui
   https://www.youtube.com/c/AmandaGatesFengShui/videos

Courses: Learn Feng Shui
   http://courses.gatesinteriordesign.com

ABOUT THE AUTHOR

Amanda Gates is an international teacher, speaker, author, and CEO and founder of Gates Interior Design. She believes that through understanding the power of energy, everyone can live a more joyful existence. Living in harmony with your surroundings is easy, however, many have been conditioned to believe otherwise and haven't been shown how.

Her company, Gates Interior Design, provides design that's energy aligned, helping homeowners and everyone in between to find more *ohm* from their homes. She helps them identify where energy kinks exist, removing blocks, and showing them a more soulful approach to their spaces, all while creating extraordinary beauty. As she always says, "Beautiful energy is what creates a beautiful space."

Amanda is also the founder of the advanced online course, Feng Shui for the Soul™. An intensive online program that teaches homeowners, healers, and coaches how to fearlessly embrace energy medicine and learn how to feel their way through spaces by heightening intuition. A process she calls "cultivating Chi."

Amanda's life philosophy is inspired by years of training in Tibetan Buddhism, ancient healing methods, Feng Shui, and Shamanism. She is also an avid yoga practitioner and believes meditation will solve all of life's problems.

Born in Southern California, and attending college in Northern California, she decided to move to Las Vegas, Nevada, for a hot minute, and finally settled down in Nashville, Tennessee, for the past eighteen years.

Her secret to life boils down to three things: hug a tree and get to know nature, eat more ice cream, and stop watching funny cat videos and get the cat—preferably a black and white one, because they are the key to humility, patience, and a lot of ridiculous joy.

facebook.com/GatesInteriorDesign
twitter.com/GatesInteriors
instagram.com/gatesinteriordesign

LEAVE A REVIEW

Thank you.

Thank you for reading Feng Shui for the Soul™. My wish is that you, the reader, develop a meaningful spiritual practice, and you glean greater understanding of how powerful you are. Like a new seed just planted, take time to gestate and grow into a beautiful oak tree that roots into this earth and touches Heaven with her branches, so that Heaven and Earth can collide within you. This is medicine for the soul.

My ask is that if you found this book helpful, inspirational, or educational in a positive way, that you leave feedback and share this book with others. Leave a positive review on Amazon, give me your input online, talk about it, and help others find this book with your message. Together, through community and collaboration, we all shall rise.

Love, Light, and Shui,
Amanda Gates